3784

The Business Plan

Gerald Schwetje · Sam Vaseghi

The Business Plan

How to Win
Your Investors' Confidence

With 39 Figures and 25 Tables

 Springer

Dipl.-Kfm. Gerald Schwetje
Hamburger Beratungs-Kontor GmbH & Co. KG
Neue ABC-Str. 8
20354 Hamburg
Germany
gschwetje@beratungs-kontor.de

Dr. Sam Vaseghi (Dipl. mult.)
Deloitte
Environment & Sustainability
Weidekampsgade 6
2300 Copenhagen S
Denmark
svaseghi@deloitte.com

Translation from German by Paula and Susanne Schwetje

Library of Congress Control Number: 2007932195

ISBN 978-3-540-25451-5 Springer Berlin Heidelberg New York

Springer is a part of Springer Science+Business Media

springer.com

© Springer-Verlag Berlin Heidelberg 2007

Production: LE-TEX Jelonek, Schmidt & Vöckler GbR, Leipzig
Cover-design: WMX Design GmbH, Heidelberg

SPIN 11412335   42/3180YL - 5 4 3 2 1 0   Printed on acid-free paper

Preface

The business plan is a versatile means and is not only restricted to start-ups or company founders. Big companies have more or less large staff divisions which have the task of thinking about strategic questions and their orientation in order to work out the plans for the next years.

What does this look like in mid-size or small companies, which cannot afford their own staff divisions or planning departments to compile and plan their strategy. In such a case it is the manager's or entrepreneur's task to develop a strategy, to define future plan data and to implement them.

Many mid-size or small companies fail, because they recognize market developments too late, because they do not promote the right products, because they have not thought about certain technological processes, because they have not adapted their organization in time. Many reasons can be named why such companies fail.

In a successful company business and strategic situations are thought about continually and decisions are made early enough in order to act successfully within the market. We believe the business plan to be a means for mid-size and small companies of thinking about their company and positioning it correctly within the market. More and more do small and mid-size companies also have to compete and view their markets from a global perspective. Only someone who has prepared himself thoroughly for this step stands a chance within the tough competition.

This book has helped many companies within the German market to think about their company and to position it correctly. That is the reason why we have decided to offer it on the international market as well. We believe it will encourage small and mid-size entrepreneurs to work out a strategic plan that will enable them to be successful within the market, also within the global market.

With this book we do not simply wish to introduce you to the theme of drawing up a business plan, we also wish to offer you a "book of thoughts", which – with all its questions – will motivate you to think about your company, to write down your ideas and plans and with these to find suitable strategies for making your company competitive.

This book could only be compiled with untiring effort of those people who helped us to translate and shape it. We are particularly thankful to Paula and Susanne Schwetje who spent many hours of their free time devoting their energies to translating the book. We also wish to thank Anna-Katharina Wenzel, who gave excellent support in correcting and completing the book. Last but not least, we would like to thank our families, who gave us the time to let this book become reality.

Hamburg, June 2007   Gerald Schwetje

Kopenhagen, June 2007   Sam Vaseghi

Preface to German edition

Due to the globalization of business activities and the internationalization of the capital markets, demands on internal and external company reporting have increased, primarily the reporting of future chances and risks has taken an outstanding position in this context. Against this background the publicity policies of a company have to be adjusted to structure the information conveyed with financial accounting and other media in such a way that the addressees (e.g. shareholders, investors, suppliers, creditors, employees, tax authorities, analysts, publicity) act in accordance with the set company goals. Thereby those responsible for such information policies should align their activities to the goal of increasing the company value (value reporting).

In this context the business plan presents an indispensable instrument of reporting, with which essential qualitative and quantitative company information can be documented for investors in a compact form, information regarding existing growth or risk potentials, beyond annual financial statement and report. The script at hand gives an extensive overview about the goals, concepts and instruments of an effective business plan. The practise oriented remarks are supported by a multitude of illustrative examples. The drawing up, using and updating of a business plan is clarified with know-how but easy language to founders of new businesses and managing directors of mid-size companies with respect to the latest knowledge in business studies.

I wish the excellent handbook a high circulation and the readers success when realizing the recommended strategies and concepts.

Hamburg, December 2003   o. Univ.-Prof. Dr. Carl-Christian Freidank,
                                                          Tax adviser

Table of contents

1 Necessity of planning

A business plan, in principle, can be seen as a document that commercializes your business idea as a whole towards potential investors and stakeholders. A business plan is successful if you succeed in conveying to the reader the most significant opportunities and growth capacities of your company realistically.

A business plan should justify and describe your business idea and further business development in a clear and adequate manner. It should not merely aim at emphasizing the strengths of the company, but rather at presenting a realistic portrait of its problems, risks and obstacles. In addition to this, appropriate solutions should be proposed and discussed in detail.

A business plan can be used for specific purposes. One target might be to obtain new means of investment for the development of a product or the marketing of a new product.

Basically a successful business plan has three important features:

- The short- and long-term objectives are clearly depicted,
- a careful description is given of how the objectives can be achieved in realistic general conditions and
- a description is given of how the realization of the plan will meet the expectations of the investors.

It is very important to clarify beforehand what purpose a business plan will serve and what it aims at. In general business plans are compiled either for an external or internal reason. In the following chapter we will describe these facts in more detail.

1.1 External use of a business plan

From an external point of view the business plan represents the main financing tool of your company. In addition, it serves to secure existing or planned business relations between your company and your stakeholders.

Depending on the type of financing and stakeholder relations, various aspects are weighed up and dealt with in different ways in a business plan.

1.1.1 Venture-capital financing

As a rule, venture-capital and private-equity investors nowadays only consider business cases which are well represented by a business plan.

When reading a business plan, the investors are primarily interested in good and relevant arguments that promise business growth. Furthermore, investors attach great importance to how and in which period of time a return on investment will be realized, for instance:

- through operating profit or
- by going public or
- by merger and acquisition or
- through a repurchase by the management.

In order to guarantee a high return on investment, investors pay great attention to:

- the company's success on the market,
- the feasibility of the plan in order to achieve its business objectives,
- the unique selling proposition of the products and services and
- the quality and experience of the management team.

1.1.2 Financing by bank credits

When granting credits, investment banks focus on one main question: when and how the repayment of the credits and interests will be made. In order to minimize risks, banks usually ask for securities. That is why credit applications addressed to banks   should provide more than a list of current and past annual accounts. Moreover, banks will also ask to what extent the companies are prepared for possible setbacks, and how they will be able to overcome such critical situations.

For these reasons banks more and more often demand professional business plans when considering applications for credits. Banks expect business plans to give qualified insight into: the enterprise strategy, the management, the organization, the market, the competitors, the products and the current and future financial and profit situation of the enterprise.

1.1.3   Strategic alliances

The formation of strategic alliances by young and growing companies within the framework of research projects, product design, marketing, etc. is gaining increasingly in importance. A strategic alliance is usually the consequence of:

- financial backing or
- access to well-established distribution channels.

Such an alliance may well succeed over several years for the benefit of all parties. The majority of companies, however, request a business plan before consenting to any long-term business relations or obligations within the framework of a strategic alliance.

1.1.4   Mergers and acquisitions

Acquisitions present an alternative for company expansion, while selling a company may be seen as the way out of a solvency crisis.

Companies that are looking for acquisition candidates usually request a detailed business plan that will support their evaluation and selection of the candidates.

Similarly, the acquisition candidate himself will also be interested in the long-term plans of any acquiring company, in order to ensure and protect his own interests for the future. This information is also the subject-matter of a business plan.

1.1.5   Customer and marketing relations

Winning a major customer or an agreement with a wholesaler is a particularly crucial step towards success for many growth companies.

Most big companies, however, are very reserved and precautious before starting negotiations with rather small and unknown companies. In such cases, a convincing business plan may clear doubts and prove decisive for inspiring confidence, opening negotiations and making further decisions. Hence, business plans effectively help to open doors to potential customers, markets and suppliers.

1.2   Internal use of the business plan

A business plan also serves as a valuable management tool from an internal viewpoint of the company. A systematically elaborated and regularly updated business plan, with a profound insight into all business matters, helps the management to efficiently plan the company's development and prepare the necessary modification measures in a structured way. Such a business plan can serve as a guide to the daily decision-making and as a control tool in managing the current business.

The joint realization of the business plan by the management team ensures an overall commitment to the company goals and controls. Achieving this commitment on the management level is most significant for the successful implementation of the plan.

Business plans make a significant contribution to the development of companies which have branches in different locations. By using business plans for each branch, the top management can on the one hand guarantee site-related business planning and on the other hand, continually control performance as well as the attainment of the business objectives. Furthermore, the long-term objectives of the entire company can be balanced by these indicators.

1.3   Basic types of business plans

For the majority of authors writing their first business plan, the question arises "How detailed should the business plan be?" To this question there is, unfortunately, no standard answer and no formula.

It is entirely up to you how detailed your business plan should be, and depends solely on the purpose and necessity behind it, as well as on the complexity of your specific business. In general, one distinguishes between three basic types of business plans:

- the short business plan,
- the extended business plan and
- the operational business plan.
- In the following these three types are described.

1.3.1   Short business plan

A short business plan is usually about 10 to 15 pages long. It is most suitable for young companies in an early stage of their development when, there still do not exist complex interrelations.

For a well-established company, a short business plan only makes sense if certain investment opportunities are to be roughly approved in advance, in order to prepare an extended business plan on the base of the short version later on.

Even if it is a "short" business plan, the required information should be conveyed in a complete and appropriate manner. The final goal is to convince potential investors that you understand your entrepreneurial business and the market extremely well.

1.3.2   Extended business plan

The extended business plan is usually about 20 to 40 pages long. This type of business plan describes the business issues of the company much more profoundly and more detailed than a short business plan would do.

The higher the required capital, the more interesting this type of business plan becomes. If, for example, you require 5 million Euros outside capital for the construction of a new and innovative industrial plant, i.e. you are striving for long-term credits, the preparation of an extended business plan would be advisable.

Such a business plan should contain a thorough market analysis and a revenue, cost and financial planning for a 5-year period.

1.3.3   Operational business plan

For well-established companies a business plan can serve the management team as an important operative tool, say a business guideline. Such a plan not only serves as a draft for the entire business organization, but also ensures a consistent appreciation on the part of the entire management with respect to the strategic objectives. Indeed, operational business plans are very long and detailed, usually comprising over 40 pages, in some cases even exceeding 100 pages.

1.4   Why managers don't write business plans

The increasing importance of business plans in the business environment possibly results in a recurring solicitude and reservation of business managers towards this topic. Moreover, in attempting to represent a complex topic by means of an exclusive business language and terminology, business plans deter many managers due to their very "academic" appearance.

But the aversion of many managers to business plans often is much more profound, namely that the description of the business objectives appears to be difficult and hardly suits their daily entrepreneurial activities.

Basically, the elaboration of a business plan is a great deal of work and would mean an additional task for the management. However, in an efficient organization, this task is based on the careful fulfilment of managerial activities that are already in progress or ones that are imminent.

Managers too often argue that the development of a business plan would be futile in recessionary times, since the market, i.e. the economic situation, changes rapidly and target specifications made by a business plan could be discarded overnight.

From our experience, there are two important arguments against this:

- The whole development process of the "business plan project" is at least just as valuable as the final "business plan document". The "business plan project", of course, encourages the management to reconsider and update their business objectives with the help of company-wide facts and tendencies. In addition to this, much of the information gained throughout the project (e.g. benchmarks), serves as a very valuable source for the evaluation and control of the current and future performance of the company.

- The business plan should not in fact be regarded as an "untouchable codex", which forbids and punishes any future course deviation along a multi-year plan. However, as a controlling tool, a business plan highlights such deviations from the planned course and also offers a sensitive and flexible framework for regularly updating the facts and figures. Such a tool allows you to quickly respond to market and economic changes in order to efficiently achieve your business goals.

1.5 Key questions

- *What goals are you pursuing with your business plan?*
- *What purpose should your business plan serve?*
  - *Preparation for negotiations with banks*
  - *Presentation for investors*
  - *As an internal management tool*

- *What kind of financing are you striving for and how much capital do you require?*
- *Which target groups and people do you want to approach by means of your business plan?*
- *What expectations, needs and demands do your readers have?*
- *Which type of business plan will you choose and why?*
- *Are there any reasons why you would still prefer not to write a business plan?*

2 Business plan project

Although business plans vary in their structure and content, they all have some features in common: they propose and describe business models, products or services, describe their corresponding markets, ways of production and service delivery. Indeed, external addressees of business plans usually want to know:

- who the shareholders are,
- how much capital is required,
- how and for what purpose capital is utilized,
- which type of financing will be chosen, and
- in what period of time an adequate return on investment can be realized.

Every business plan should clearly discuss these essential issues, and present them concisely and in a convincing way. The reader should be in a position to understand the business as a whole and to gain confidence in the company.

In order to deal with these issues in a sophisticated and professional manner, it is wise to draw up your business plan within the framework of a company-wide project; this we call the "business plan project".

It is not advisable to start writing a business plan when you are still unprepared as regards organization and then to expect that everything will be compiled and explained by itself. Instead, sound project planning should precede the development of the business plan.

As shown in figure 2.1 the business plan project is usually structured into five phases:

- Data collection
- Data analysis
- Design of the business plan

Fig. 2.1. Phases of the business plan project.

- Drawing-up of the business plan
- Presentation of the business plan.

The business plan should be structured into clearly defined sections. These sections should show the different aspects of your business i.e. your company. The compilation of a structure forces the management to decide at an early stage of the process where the different topics should be positioned and discussed. Inappropriate structuring is a common weakness of many business plans. Furthermore, sophisticated structuring demands of the management to consider very carefully in advance how detailed the different sections of the business plan should be.

In general, the sections of a business plan correspond to different business fields:

- Management and organization,
- Products and services,
- Market and competition,
- Marketing and sales,
- Research and development,
- Production,
- Procurement and logistics and
- Finances.

Imagine that each of these sections or areas has its own partial business plan. Provided that data collection is carried out once over all areas at the beginning of the project, the process of compiling each partial plan would be sub-divided into four phases:

- Data analysis for a specific area,
- Design of the partial plan for a specific area,

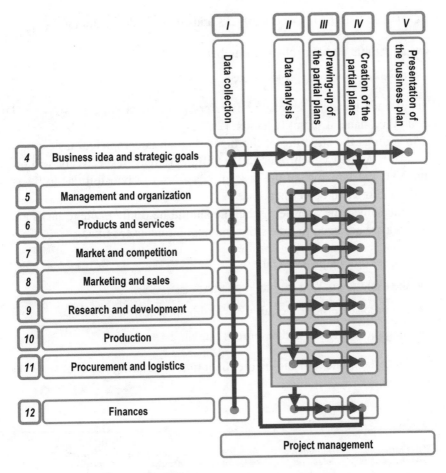

Fig. 2.2. The roadmap of the business plan project.

- Drawing-up of the partial plan for a specific area and
- Presentation of the partial plan for a specific area.

In order to illuminate the process of the entire business plan project, a roadmap is illustrated in the figure 2.2.

Herein the building blocks in the left column correspond to chapters 4 to 12 of this book.

Starting with an overall data collection, the arrows point to the different project milestones. The Roman numbering of the columns refers to the project phases, whereas the Arabic numbering of the lines refers to the sections, respectively to the appropriate chapters of this book.

Conclude that the respective blocks and stops are designated to:

- an Arabic number (chapter number) as well as
- a Roman number (project phase).

For instance the designation (12-I) refers to the data collection phase (I) within the financial sector (Chapter 12).

As soon as the structure of the business plan is completed, task groups should be defined which refer to the different areas, respectively sections (fig. 2.3). The structure of the task groups allows responsibilities to be assigned and roles to be defined.

At the same time a project schedule should be drafted, where tasks and activities are assigned to time slots and appointments are fixed.

- the set up of a project team,
- the assignment of a project manager,
- the precise definition of all roles and responsibilities,
- the precise project and resources planning

in order to facilitate a disciplined collaboration, assuring the quality of the entire process.

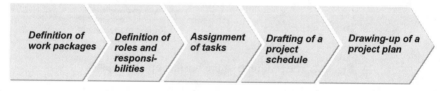

Fig. 2.3. The development of the project plan.

Before starting the project, the work packages, the activities and the responsibilities and timelines should be well communicated and covered by all project team members. This could be done by an opening meeting (kick off).

Indeed, it is not recommended to engage external consultants for the preparation of a business plan. The engagement of external consultants, of course, may seem to save precious time, however, investors and analysts recognize quite quickly whether a business plan was written by an entrepreneur himself or by a professional consultant; they would usually prefer the former and reject the latter. Temporarily, however, independent consultants could be engaged for reviews in order to evaluate the plan or excerpts of it from the viewpoint of an independent expert.

2.1 Data collection

An effective business plan requires a high data quality. In an overall company-wide action, all relevant data should be collected (Stops 11.I to 4.I of the roadmap in fig. 2.2) into one data pool.

Whenever analysts and investors encounter essential information about your industry, your market or your technology, which has not been included in your business plan, you can be certain that they will doubt the reliability of the complete plan.

The entire business plan project will run more effectively and faster, if data is collected in a structured way across all business areas. This approach would have the advantage that intermittent data completion during the subsequent project phases could be almost completely avoided.

The basic data required for a business plan is represented by the listing below; of course the specific requirements of a company may vary from this and require reductions or further extensions.

Company description

- Company name
- Legal form
- Location
- Date of foundation
- Company history
- Location of the subsidiaries
- Name of the shareholders
- Key financial data (e.g. revenue and profit of the last 3 years)
- Number of employees in the last 3 years

Management team and organization

- Organization chart
- Key management and board of directors
- Age structure of the board members

- Company affiliation of the managers
- Responsibilities and competencies of the management team
- Key members of the employees' committee
- Number of employees
- Compensation and other employee agreements

Products and services

- Product catalogue
  - Sales volume in the last 3 years
  - Revenue in the last 3 years
  - Costs in the last 3 years
  - Profit margins in the last 3 years
- Product descriptions and technical specifications
- Planned product launches
- Advertising and promotion tools
- Pricing schedules
- Competitive advantages
- Unique selling propositions
- Patents, licenses and trademarks and their terms of use
- Regulations and industrial standards

Market and competition

- Market size and social trends
- Customers and patterns of demand
- Results of customer satisfaction surveys
- Competitors
- Goals and strategies of the individual competitors
- Comparative advantages and disadvantages of your company in comparison with the main competitors

Marketing and sales

- Information per product line

- – Market share in the last *3* years
- – Planned sales volume (*5* years)
- – Planned revenue (*5* years)
- – Marketing costs
- – Profit margins
- Marketing tools
- Structure of sales department

Development and production

- Number of the production locations
- Number of workers in the last *3* years
- Applied manufacturing processes
- Alteration of the warehouse stocks in the last *3* years
- Share of development costs of the last *3* years' turnover
- List of all product launches during the last *3* years

Procurement and logistics

- Information about subcontractors
  - – Coordinates
  - – Name
  - – Type of supplied goods
- Supplier contracts and agreements
- Name of logistics agents
- Development of the internal and external haulage of the last *3* years

Finance

- Annual financial statements and controls of the last *3* years
- Financial planning, forecast, for the current year with all respective assumptions
- Required investments and timeline
- Credit lines
- Loan agreements
- Evolution of key performance indicators (KPIs) within the last *3* years

2.2   Initial analysis of the data

When data collection has been completed, a preliminary data analysis (stops to 4.II of the roadmap in fig. 2.2) would illuminate an overall portrait of your company and the current state of your business. The data raised in the different areas should be reviewed, structured and top-down analysed by the management team.

Particular attention should be paid to the analysis of the current situation; this is the initial situation, which, of course, determines the future development of the company.

This analysis should allow the management to found the business idea and plan the strategic goals at a pretentious level. We will come back to this issue in the chapter 4 of this book.

The data analysis should also provide an estimate, whether the capacities and general resources for the realization of the business idea already exist or still have to be planned and developed.

If the company does not exist yet, the initial data have to be partially gathered by external research, e.g. benchmarks etc.

An important step within this phase is the preparation of a preliminary draft of the executive summary. On the basis of the collected data, the business idea, the planning of the strategic goals, as well as the content structure of the business plan, you would be able to draft your executive summary. This first draft could then be recurrently revised and improved during the next project phases in order to achieve a mature executive summary at the end of the project. It should be mentioned that although this type of approach diverges from the traditional procedure, where an executive summary is written at the end of the entire project, we encourage everybody to do so. This issue is discussed in chapter 3 of this book, where also the advantages of our approach are highlighted.

2.3   Partial plans

In the next step the strategic plan, which determines both the core business idea as well as the strategic goals, should be communicated to the teams, which are responsible for the different sections and areas (stops 5.IV to 10.II of the roadmap in figure 2.2).

The corresponding work packages will be delegated by the management toward the area managers, their project managers and task forces, who are responsible for working out the partial plans within a committed period of time and delivering the final documents to the management in order to analyse the common financial impact.

Within the framework of the business plan project you should organize workshops which facilitate a structured exchange of experience and knowledge between the different area teams and task forces. The efficient realization of the workshops is crucial for the harmonisation of the partial plans and the final success of the entire business plan project. The workshops make it possible to identify and coordinate interrelations and dependencies between different divisions. A good example of such a critical dependency is the relation between organizational planning and the different objectives of the other areas, e.g. marketing, production etc.

All partial plans should be aligned to the strategic plan as communicated by the management.

2.4 Financial plan and control

In further step the partial plans are compiled, consolidated and in their entirety examined in regard to financial impact and feasibility.

On the basis of this consolidation a cross-functional financial plan could be created (stops 12.II to 12.IV of the roadmap in figure 2.2). The development of the financial plan is described in chapter 12. The financial plan has to be aligned with the objectives of the different areas as well we as with the strategic plan and goals. If the financial plan deviates from the strategic plan, the management must be informed immediately so that they are able to act quickly.

In such a case two alternatives exist:

- The strategic plan cannot be kept partially and should be revised and adapted appropriately by the management.

- The partial plans or their interrelations do not allow an appropriate alignment with the strategic goals and should be revised by the task forces.

This way of review gives rise to an iterative approach which can be controlled by the project management. The supervision by the management ensures a recurring improvement of the entire business plan (stops 4.I to 4.II of the roadmap in figure 2.2). Each iteration step is of course accompanied by a repeated revision and optimization of the executive summary (chapter 3).

By means of these tactics you will finally achieve a mature and conclusive business plan.

In addition, this procedure ensures that your business plan will communicate the core business idea, the strategic goals and objectives and the basics of the operative plans stepwise into your company organization. This process increases the willingness and motivation of the management as well as the employees with regard to the later realization of the resultant measures.

2.5 Key questions

- *Have you identified the potential readers of the business plan and chosen a type of business plan that will fit their requirements?*
- *Have you already defined the sections of your business plan and the corresponding content structure?*
- *Have you already prepared the structure of the partial plans as well as the required data related to the sections? Have you prepared standardized document templates?*
- *Have you set up the roadmap for the preparation of your business plan?*
- *Have you already reached an agreement within the management team on research, preparations and feedback?*
- *Are the sections and the corresponding work packages well defined and represented?*
- *Are the roles and responsibilities within the framework of the project clearly defined and communicated?*
- *Are the most important project milestones well defined and a project plan set up?*
- *Have you planned sufficient time and resources for data collection and analysis in common agreement with the managers and project team members?*
- *Have you planned the necessary resources for the project?*
- *Have you carefully prepared the kick off meeting (agenda, topics, goals, participants, communication, etc.)?*
- *Have you defined the role of the consultants you wish to involve in your project?*

- *Which tasks and responsibilities of the project are addressed to you in person?*

- *What resistance will you encounter during enforcement of your project and its objectives on different hierarchy levels?*

- *Have you already elaborated an overall check list for data acquisition?*

- *Are external data sources also requested for your business plan?*

- *Which analysis tools (SWOT, brainstorming, portfolio, decision trees, fish diagrams, etc.) will you apply in order to analyse the overall data?*

- *Have you already developed a qualified concept for the workshops?*

- *If you are already in the second round of the project, which data were missing in the first round of the preparation of the executive summary and the business plan?*

3   Executive summary

The executive summary compiles the essential statements and conclusions of your business plan in a very concise form. For the majority of readers the executive summary will present the most important section of the business plan, because:

- it ensures a quick introduction into the main topics,
- it gives a short overview of your enterprise.
- it provides the investor with the core statements and conclusions of your enterprise strategy and success factors.

Investors, bankers and representatives of investment groups get lots of business plans on their desks every day. Indeed, they may not read the whole documents. But they usually read the executive summary first, in order to quickly check, whether a review of the complete document would be worthwhile.

Provided the executive summary sounds promising, the reader will feel encouraged to read the whole business plan. On the other hand, if the executive summary does not convince at first sight, even a good business plan could be rejected. Hence, avoid postponing the essential information to the later sections of your business plan, as most readers will not give you another chance if the main concerns are not already embodied in the executive summary.

Figures and facts resulting from your data analysis (chapter 2) must be perfectly represented. Otherwise, readers will doubt and question the plausibility of your whole business plan. However, if you are reliant on estimated data in your executive summary, you should provide the investor with convincing arguments and clear formulations in order to avoid raising any kind of scepticism.

3.1   Key to an effective executive summary

What makes an executive summary an effective tool?

First of all, it is important to know that an executive summary does not serve as a preface or introduction to the business plan. It is rather the elaboration of an explicit summary of the entire business plan.

The reader should be able to read and understand the executive summary independently of the rest of the business plan. The investor should understand the points of your business plan merely by reading the executive summary.

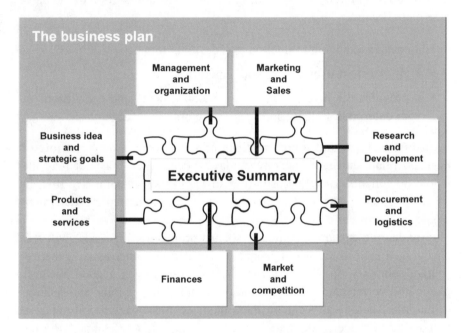

Fig. 3.1. Information sources of the executive summary.

An effective executive summary includes all the key elements of a business plan on just two or three pages. It should include the following essential information:

An outline of the enterprise strategy with emphasis on the success factors: With your executive summary you provide the reader with a short survey of your strategic goals, your business idea (chapter 4) and key data relevant to success, e.g. revenue, profit and profitability (appendix 1) in the last three years, as well as your plan for the next five years.

A presentation of the key qualifications of the management team which will guarantee the success of the company: Make sure that you describe the contribution your team will make to successful business initiatives. The investor is interested in the structure of your management team and their qualifications.

A short description of the market, the success formula and unique selling propositions on the market: You must convince the investor that your products and innovations will prove to be competitive on the relevant market. Therefore, it is especially important to know your target market, its trends, the needs and preferences of your customers and the services provided by your competitors.

A concise presentation of your competitive advantages: Show in brief with which strategies you operate successfully on your market and how you have already distinguished yourself from your competitors and intend to do so in future. Explain your operative strategies (manufacturing, procurement, logistics and marketing) to your investor in a few sentences.

A short description of the products and services: Describe your products and services and thereby mention the essential features, in particular the unique selling propositions. It is also possible to first refer to the exceptional features in the choice and compilation of your product portfolio. Explain your production technology, product development and the arising expenses involved with them

Reference to your communication methods: Briefly mention which communication methods you use to increase public awareness of the product and to position your product in the relevant market.

Key financial data: Here you should give an insight into relevant financial data, e.g. annual revenue, sales volumes and costs for a period of three to five years.

The description of your financial requirements: This demands an estimate of the required financial resources, an explanation of how you wish to use these, and how and when you will guarantee repayment to your investors.

The structure and design of an effective executive summary is one of the most difficult tasks facing a manager when drawing up a business plan.

Try in advance to show the reader your short-term and long-term company goals, or rather the success factors in your company. Using the system shown in figure 3.2., formulate which measures you will take to achieve these goals in your company.

In phrasing the core statement, you should first define the goal i.e. the benefit for your company, and then coordinate the verb of action to your benefit. Subsequently, you should consider which measures have to be determined to achieve this benefit.

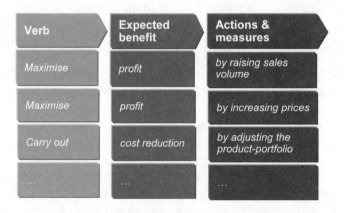

Verb	Expected benefit	Actions & measures
Maximise	profit	by raising sales volume
Maximise	profit	by increasing prices
Carry out	cost reduction	by adjusting the product-portfolio
...	...	...

Fig. 3.2. Basic scheme for the formulation of the key statements.

3.2   Executive summary and the business plan

You cannot expect the first version of the executive summary, which you have worked out in an early phase of the project, to be the final one. You should be prepared to revise the executive summary after the first structuring of the business plan. In an early stage of developing the business plan the provisional version of the executive summary merely serves the following purposes:

It serves as a conceptual guideline for the business plan. While developing the executive summary you will be forced to think about the most essential elements of the business plan more closely. Furthermore, you will have to assign priorities to your different aims, in other words to distinguish the important aims from the less important ones, because only the significant ones should be included in the executive summary.

It creates self-confidence in yourself as well as confidence in your business plan. If you gather the key elements of your business plan carefully together within the framework of the executive summary, you will prevent writing blockades and delays from occurring at a later date, such blockades and delays that arise from repeatedly losing one's bearings while developing the business plan. A brief collection of the most important points allows you to develop a feeling for the course and objectives.

It involves the management team in the planning procedures right from the start. The drawing up of a first version of the executive summary is an effective way of integrating the members of the management team in the analyses. The joint forces of the management team ensure a valuable contribution to the content of the business plan as well as early agreement about the objectives.

It leads to a better final product. Repeated writing is the key to successful writing. An executive summary, which sets the course for the elaboration of the whole business plan, should again be revised thoroughly at the end of the process. To draw a conclusion, the result would be a better business plan as well as a better executive summary.

As soon as you have completely elaborated all the other components of the business plan, you should devote yourself to the executive summary again. First, make sure that the content and statements of the executive summary correspond with all the information and details of the other parts. Take heed of the points mentioned above. The next step is to question yourself if the executive summary shows clearly that:

- the business has been investigated and planned thoroughly,

- the business model is reasonable and useful,

- a sound understanding of the products' and services' contribution to the value has been created,

- your business plans do in fact produce competitive advantages,

- there exists a profound knowledge of the industry and the target markets,

- you and your team will tackle the business with enthusiasm, and

- a realistic picture of the business risks has been worked out.

Provided you express these key messages powerfully and precisely together with the important content aspects previously described, the reader will get a profound understanding of your strategies, plans and goals. Figure 3.3 again sums up what you have to pay attention to when drawing up a convincing executive summary.

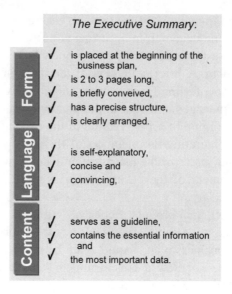

Fig. 3.3. Main requirements of an executive summary.

3.3   Advantages of an executive summary

An effective executive *summary* is supportive in two respects when seeking a funding source:

- **It serves as a summary of the core statements of the business plan and defends the business idea.** If your business plan is very long and detailed, it will be difficult to approach the reader directly. If you should send your business plan to credit granters or investors who do not know you and who perhaps have no immediate interest in your offer, it would then be more advisable to approach them with only the executive summary of your business plan and an accompanying letter for the time being. Should those who have any say in the matter be interested in the complete business plan after reading the executive summary, you could then forward or even present it to them personally. This procedure enables you not to reveal any confidential details of your business.

- **The readers are involved.** A clearly worked out and convincing executive summary will ensure that your business plan stands out against the masses of other business plans, and will encourage the reader to want to find out more about your company and what is behind your business idea.

3.4 Key questions

- *Are all essential data and information available for a concise description of the key elements of your executive summary (budget, strategy, product, distribution etc.)?*

- *Have you formulated your business goals as precise core statements?*

- *Does your executive summary meet all formal, language and content requirements?*

- *If you are in the second round of the project, have you revised your executive summary in accordance with the first draft of your business plan?*

4 Business idea and strategic goals

4.1 Business idea

Every company emerges from a business idea; but a promising idea must be more than just a wish to sell products or services.

One has to tackle a business idea intensively in order to advance it and make it a true business objective. In many conversations with entrepreneurs and founders we perceive again and again that the business idea is either described insufficiently or not at all. A good idea is far from being automatically a good business idea. We often find that scientists, for instance, being quite convinced of a discovery they have made, hardly ever have any idea of approaching the market.

When considering business ideas, you should write these ideas down and try to define them in detail. In doing this, you should refer to further sources like magazines, the internet or interviews. You should discuss your idea with entrepreneurs or consultants who are well-known to you, in order to illuminate the idea from different perspectives. At this point you often realize that others have already taken up or even realized the idea. This often is the moment the idea is dismissed and disappears from the scene. It is a frustrating moment when you notice that the obstacle appears too high and the idea cannot be realized. You simply give up! This behaviour is understandable, but unfortunate and basically inconsequent: for it is precisely this obstacle that presents the first challenge, which leads you to continually develop your business idea. Do not allow yourself to give up your idea so easily and regain the conviction that you are pursuing an interesting idea. Think of all those shining examples that held on to their ideas firmly and without wavering. The brilliant inventor Gottlieb Daimler, for instance, was at first employed as a leading engineer by the then renowned gas engine manufacturer Deutz. He soon realized the enormous technical and economical potential of the four-stroke engine and looked for various means of applying it. To him it was not the engine itself that was the significant factor, but the diverse possibilities of employing it. In 1885 he developed the first motorcycle, in 1886 there followed a motorboat, his famous motor coach as well as further employment of the engine as a railcar or the controllable balloon driven by propellers. Daimler held his own against many odds, continued working consistently on his ideas and thus set the foundation stone of one of the most successful companies in Germany. Model entrepreneurs always succeed in their intentions against many odds through their pragmatic and critical insight, and they do not reap the fruits of their work, namely entrepreneurial success, until many years later.

Business ideas emerge in many different ways. It may be a question of a new product, new rules in an existing business model, or only the imitation of other companies, taking advantage of discernible weaknesses. In order to make this clear, we will show you a further example.

In the year *1836,* after many years of experimenting, the joiner Michael Thonet devised the bending of wood by heating the wood in a glue bath. With this method he produced the chairs and armchairs made of curved wood, for which his company later became famous. Thonet was also one of the first entrepreneurs who put a stamp on the frames of his chairs in order to protect them against imitators. When twenty years later the chair making craft had become a chair manufacturing industry, the chairs received an emblem in the form of a sun with eight rays. Thus Thonet furniture became one of the first branded products.

The idea of standardizing and industrializing craftsmen's work was the idea that often stood at the beginning of successful enterprise stories and of trade development e.g.

- from tailoring to clothing brands,
- from the butcher's shop to the sausage factory,
- from the baker's shop to the breads and pastries concern, or
- from the sawmill to the prefabricated house manufacturer.

Other successful business ideas existed and exist in:

- making brands out of anonymous products as foods, cosmetic articles, medicines;
- standardizing services and making them nationally available: all franchise retail systems, the cleaning of buildings, transport agencies, fast food chains;
- developing new technologies: substituting glass lenses with silicon ones, replacing beverage receptacles made of glass and tin with paper ones, using composites instead of steel, replacing tubes with flat screens and cable connections with radio networks, etc.;

- offering products with little or no service included; all types of self-service, cheap airlines;

- finding new markets or sales channels: direct marketing, food at service stations, market places and product auctions via internet;

- changing the production scale: carrying out only final assembly, purchasing product components;

- reducing the range of services – along the value-added chain: hiving off administration services, agreeing to alliances with competitors and hiving off production and logistics completely.

The business idea can (or sometimes even has to) change in the course of time because the customers' wishes change or because new technologies replace old procedures. The company Thonet, for instance, began with the additional production of tubular steel furniture after having come in contact with top designers of Bauhaus.

4.2 Business model

Business ideas are developed by very different motivations. Many people may have ideas but only few accomplish the final realization of a business idea.

Remember how Bill Gates, the founder of *Microsoft*, developed an operating system in his garage, unaware of the fact that his business idea would one day become a dominating product worldwide. His idea of developing an operating system did not mature to a business until *IBM* charged him with the development of an operating system for the *IBM PC*. Of course, *IBM* was his greatest coup. He thus found a customer who was ready to pay him a price for his services.

His business idea and his customer secured him his turnover. This enabled Bill Gates to found his company *Microsoft*. His business model (fig. 4.1) resulted from the business idea and the revenue model.

In order to develop a business model, you must consider from the very beginning who would be prepared to pay a price for your business idea. There are two conditions you have to check:

- what product or service justifies your business idea, and

- what revenue you can realize with your product or service.

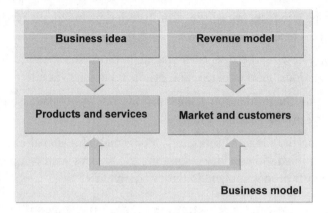

Fig. 4.1. The business model.

When you have developed your business idea, you have to check if you can find a target customer who is prepared to pay a price for your services. Only then can you think about writing a business plan. That means you should consider your idea intensively. You should ask yourself:

- what business you run
- why you run it
- what advantage and benefit you offer
- how you distinguish yourself from your competitors
- which customers you want to attract
- which customer needs you fulfil and how
- what products you manufacture
- how you manufacture and distribute these products
- which profit and growth you aim at
- with which methods you want to achieve success

When you have defined your business model, you should describe it briefly and precisely. Investors, through experience, will very quickly recognize the quality and substance of a business model.

This is also valid for existing enterprises, as their business models also change and you constantly have to adapt to new challenges, too.

4.3   Strategic goals

Based on the business model, the company strategy can now be derived. This company strategy allows you to develop the strategic goals right up to the operational ones.

First of all, describe your company model (fig. 4.2) by means of your business model, through which your products and your services can be defined. Then present your market and the customers to whom you want to sell your products and services. Remember that the target customers will only be willing to pay the price if products and services correspond to their benefit expectations. Furthermore, your products and services determine the tasks in your company. With them you will lay the foundations for calculating and planning your resources and costs.

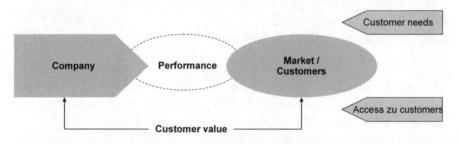

Fig. 4.2. The company model.

The *customer value* is determined by the products and services you provide the customer with. Your products and services help the customer to fulfil a need. The customer value can also consist of a unique selling proposition or a significant economic advantage.

A company strategy can be defined as the way to a destination that you as an entrepreneur define from the very beginning of your venture. In many middle class companies we are faced with the following situation: if we ask what they intend to do in the next three years, we are inundated with ideas and strategies; however, if we ask whether they have documented or communicated this in their company, we receive the simple answer, "We have this stored in our minds; we can't possibly write it all down, since the markets change so quickly."

Here lies the crux of the matter! It would be much wiser to think over one's business idea and the strategic direction of one's company and set that down in a business plan. Remember, investors want to understand why you run your business and why they are to invest in your company. Goals and strategies showing how the future business will be carried out are particularly important. The growth of an enterprise must be plausible from its historical beginning right into its future.

In order to be able to develop goals and strategies, it is wise to know what you want; for only if you know what you want, can you formulate a strategic direction. Therefore, you should develop an idea of your future company outline. From a strategic point of view this is a vision, a long-term perspective. Long-term perspectives are always elusive, but one thing is sure: the world is changing and you want to make money with your business model in future, too. Hence it is important to think about this long-term perspective. On the basis of your vision, you define your business purpose, your mission. Only when you have done this, should you start formulating your strategic and operative goals.

4.3.1 Vision

Let us begin with the long-term perspective: what do you want to achieve in 5 to 10 years. Develop a future picture of your enterprise. We do not want to open an academic discussion, but merely to emphasize the strengths of a vision. The French pilot, writer and visionary Antoine de Saint-Exupery, once described his vision of building a ship as follows: "If you want to build a ship, don't drum up people together to collect wood and don't assign them tasks and work, but rather teach them to long for the endless immensity of the sea."

A vision describes the future picture of your enterprise. The vision must be desirable, challenging, but also attainable, otherwise, rather than strengthen creativity within your enterprise, it will cause frustration. Visions formulated clearly and simply will encourage the creativity of your people.

Henry Ford was a visionary of his time, when he developed the "Model-T". At that time many designing engineers worked on the development of cars, convinced of making money only with luxury cars and sports cars for the rich. Henry Ford thought differently and had a vision: developing a motor vehicle which, through standardization and mass production, could be offered so cheaply that affording a car became possible for many people. Nothing would divert Ford from this vision and he put it into practice. This was the birth of one of the world's leading car manufacturers.

Without visions enterprises, as a rule, fail at the slightest signs of change, or they decline into destructive compromises.

4.3.2   Mission

The vision delivers the "subject" of your enterprise. The mission describes the purpose of the enterprise, its strategies, behaviour patterns and values. In the so called *mission statement* you should briefly and precisely describe your company, explain what you would like to do and how you will be able to assert yourself in competition with other companies.

In 1973, the probably most well-known international management guru, Peter Drucker, wrote in his management book "Tasks, Responsibilities, Practices" that the fact that an enterprise's purpose and task are rarely thought over in an adequate manner, might be the most significant reason for the failure and breakdown of a company.

The task of an enterprise may lie in the manufacturing of products that provide benefits for a target group, for instance the production of Aspirin, or in the supply of services in health care, as for instance the medical services of a general practitioner. Describe your business purpose briefly and precisely, also what you are focusing on, and clearly define your tasks. The business purpose gives a third party insight into what you are aiming at. You should also point out in a mission statement, which strategic direction you are pursuing.

Apart from the description of the original business purpose and the strategic direction, you should also formulate your company values. They give an insight into your enterprise culture and show how you intend to work together with those who are interested in your company. Not only investors are interested in this, but also shareholders, employees, directors, customers and suppliers.

Just how strongly the code of conduct affects an enterprise can be shown by the example of IBM. Buck Rogers formulated the code of conduct of an IBM'er as follows, that everyone at IBM works in marketing and every employee is trained to respect the customer as the most important priority. Everyone means every one – beginning with the executive board via the finance department down to the reception and the employees in IBM production. Indeed IBM is one of the most successful sales organizations in the world.

In 1914 Tom Watson, the founder of IBM, formulated a code of conduct that was clearly understandable for everybody, and with it defined the value system of IBM. The basic principles were as follows:

- Respect for the individual.
- Best possible service toward the customer.

- Aiming at excellent performance.
- Even today IBM works and thinks according to these principles.

4.3.3 Company goals

You have now formulated your vision and mission and know what you want. Hence it is time to derive clear goals from these, goals which you set and pursue, and which are understandable for a third party. Remember: if you know what you want, you can formulate your strategic direction and thus your goals.

Strategic goals are usually targets you would like to achieve within the next 3 *to* 5 years. Such goals may be:

- profit
- revenue
- growth
- market shares
- specific customers or customer groups
- products and services
- product design
- production, capacities and locations
- investments
- suppliers

Furthermore, your strategies, as well as your tactical objectives related to products, sales, development, production etc., are both based on your strategic goals (fig. 4.3).

You should define your goals and targets by means of the following criteria:

- reasons for these goals and targets,
- height of these goals and targets, and
- time schedule for these goals and targets

so that they can be checked at any time.

Fig. 4.3. The target hierarchy in an enterprise.

Table 4.1. Example for the definition of goals and targets.

Goal	Description of the goals	Target value	Measurement
Revenue	Return on total sales as the sum of the project business' revenues, esspecially:		
	- Total revenue - Revenue of the sales areas - Average revenue of the service areas - Average revenue per employee	-€ 50 Mio - Thd. - Tbd. - € 200.00	- Annual Sales - Revenue report of S.A. - Revenue report of S.A. - Revenue report of E.
Profit	Profitability figures esspecially:		
	- EBIT - EBIT of the industry	-20% -Tbd.	- Annual/quater/month P&L - Annual/quater/month P&L; analysis per industry
	- Operational minimum project margins	-Min. 30 % profit margin	- Project controlling
Growth	Annual increase of the main business figures, average growth (CAGR) over 5 years - Revenue	- 35 % p.a.	- P & L

When you define targets, keep in mind that they should be realisable. Table 4.1 shows an example of how one can elaborate concrete target values and control instruments from the strategic goals.

Your set of targets will now provide the framework for your business plan as described in the chapters 5 to 12. In each of the chapters the goals are adjusted to the historical evolution of the business and the future course of your business.

4.4   Key questions

- *What is your business idea?*
- *To what extent are your business ideas realistic and acceptable?*
- *What are your products and services?*
- *How can marketable products and services be derived from your business idea?*
- *How can your revenue model be described?*
- *How can your business model be described?*
- *How can your company model be represented?*
- *How can your business and enterprise model be checked?*
- *Have you already got a vision for your company?*
- *Have you already described a mission for your company?*
- *What are the purposes of your company?*
- *Why do you run your company?*
- *Which strategy do you pursue?*
- *How can you achieve strategic positions which will bring a competitive advantage for your company?*
- *Which values have you developed for your company?*
- *Are the values in accordance to your company strategy?*
- *Which code of conduct have you defined?*
- *Does the statement deliver a portrait of the company and match the company culture?*
- *Is the statement easily readable and intelligible?*
- *Which potential customers can you win?*
- *What do your customers require of your products and services?*
- *Are your customers willing to pay a price for your products and services?*
- *Do you know any customers with whom you could test and talk about the products?*
- *What are your strategic goals?*

- *Have you already reached a market share? Which one?*
- *What are your future ideas? Which size do you want to reach?*
- *Are your growth and profit targets realistic with regard to the market trends and your competitors?*
- *What distinguishes your business model from that of your main competitors?*
- *How sustainable are your technologies?*
- *Which investment requirements do you have?*

5 Management team and organization

Investors increasingly focus on the quality of the management team:

- its technical and industry specific qualifications,
- its entrepreneurial experience,
- its integrity, as well as the commitment and skills of each individual manager.

What is more important than the organization chart is the presentation of the key personnel and their skills and expertise.

The assessment of the management and their ability to manage a variety of different market and company situations plays a particularly important role. In this context everything depends on the management's experience in leadership and in dealing with crises, as well as their knowledge of the industry. The description of the management and the organization might be very subjective. Therefore, you should pay particular attention to the topic.

In this chapter we would like to deal with the main aspects of company organization and management. Having already taken a critical look at the strategic goals of your company, we can now consider the following questions: How can you achieve your goals, and what resources do you need to achieve these objectives?

You can only answer these questions, if you have a definite and plausible idea of the different tasks your company faces and if you make it perfectly clear to yourself how you plan to structure your company, bearing in mind the various workflows, activities and resources. Thus we will first consider the so-called operational structure of your company and then determine its organizational structure.

Finally we will turn to the topic of how to organize and structure your management team.

5.1 Operational structure

Based on the description of your business idea, your business model and your strategic goals, you can present your operational structure. This will require an overriding and not too detailed description of the main work-flows along your value chain.

This leads us to the way in which you plan to:

- construct your products and service channels
- include the products and services of third parties
- market your products, and
- manage the cross-functional organization of workflows.

By means of these issues you can establish the most significant operational activities of your enterprise and start planning the required resources, people, work material and systems.

In doing this, it is important to ensure an overall insight into the market, your target customers. Furthermore, you should have an idea about which products and services you wish to market to which customers. You should also determine production facilities and services as well as precursor materials required. These steps will serve as a guideline for organizing your company.

In many cases investors have only limited understanding of the organizational interrelations and tend to judge the financial situation of your company mainly with regard to the balance sheets. Yet it is precisely your company's organizational presentation which the investors can derive from how efficiently and effectively your company really works.

This applies to start-ups and their founders likewise, for it is through the presentation of the operational structure that you can show how explicitly you have considered the internal workflows. In a next step you can plan the resources effectively, which in turn makes the planning and the related expenditures appear plausible and convincing to a third party.

Yet how does one assess the operational structure of an enterprise? The operational structure covers the organization of the entire operational processes in a company. It can be defined as sequences of logically related activities or operational steps which are performed within a certain period of time. Thereby, information or materials (e.g. raw materials, forms, phone calls) are applied to a certain work force unit as Input and, in order to achieve added value, are transformed into Output through consecutive activities.

Begin with a rough structure of your value chain from the customer's point of view (important!) and structure the workflows from the acquisition via incoming orders to the purchase of your raw or precursor materials:

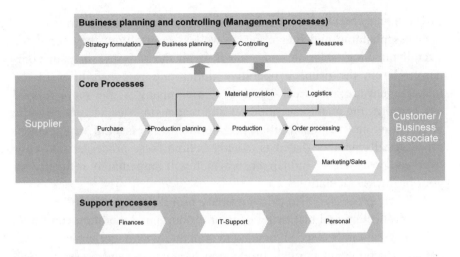

Fig. 5.1. Example of a *high level process model*.

For this purpose you should develop a so-called *High Level Process Model,* also referred to as *process map*, in which you additionally describe your customers, suppliers and cooperation partners.

The process map can help you to present a structured overview of your operational processes. Usually one distinguishes between three different process groups:

- Management processes,
- core processes and
- support processes.

These three types should be analysed and presented in a clear and concise way. Certainly, every company operates in a different way and we can address only general aspects and show common principles. In your own business plan, of course, you should follow the operational structures and processes of your own company from a helicopter perspective. Do avoid elaborating a complete organizational manual, hundreds of pages illustrated with complex process diagrams, and all sub-processes, workflows and activities!

In many companies we observe again and again that the operational processes are still not well understood and documented, and the organizational representation is only carried out by means of an organization chart. Of course, that does not suffice to convince an experienced reader of the company's organizational capabilities.

The management processes describe the development of a strategy, the business planning and budgeting as well as controlling; they serve the overall planning, steering and control of all the activities in your company. Herein the primary operative duties and responsibilities of the management are anchored. The bigger a company is, the more refined and complex the management duties and responsibilities become. Bundle your duties and responsibilities and define your essential management processes. Remember that it is exactly behind these processes that your overhead costs will be hidden, costs which will immediately influence all your business calculations.

The core processes, also called primary processes, are directly involved in the production and marketing of your products and therefore contribute to value creation. It is recommended to structure your entire business process from acquisition through production to purchase and assess at each stage whether the process is still promising. Leading technical changes, for example the introduction of new machines, restructuring of the business processes, or the structuring of customer activities, may result in quite new processes and operational structures, which would influence the efficiency of your organization significantly. During the assessment of the core processes new ideas and starting points often arise in order to introduce changes and improvements. Only if you pay particular attention to your operational processes or your value chain, will you be able to improve and optimize the processes within your company towards a competitive edge. This might be your core competences, competences which you will continuously have to improve and adapt to market challenges.

The support processes or so called infrastructural processes include information management, personnel, accounting and finance. Although these processes are not directly linked to the value chain, they basically support the core processes and facilitate the overall operational performance of your company. These processes, too, should be frequently assessed, since they also contribute to overhead costs. The question that could here be posed is whether or not support processes can be outsourced. For small and medium-sized enterprises (SMEs), for instance, it could be advantageous to outsource services like financial and payroll accounting to tax accountants or common service providers. Furthermore, the information management should be appropriately assessed as to whether or not it can partly or entirely be outsourced. Founders should seriously consider outsourcing these types of services from the very beginning in order to concentrate on their core business activities.

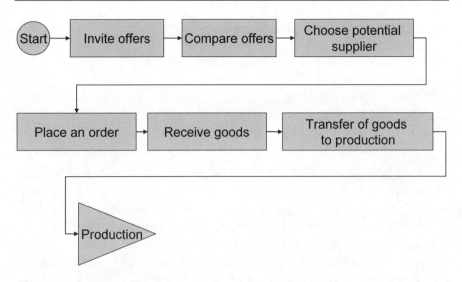

Fig. 5.2. Example of a procurement process.

Behind your comprehensive presentation of the processes, there exist, of course, further detailed sub-processes, which become apparent at a further level. Develop and describe these critical sub-processes in their workflows and activities. This will help you to efficiently assess and analyse opportunities for further improvement and optimization. In fig. 5.2 a simplified procurement process with related sub-processes is shown.

Following fig 5.2 in particular you could break down the existing activity blocks into further building blocks and conclude the required resources, people and materials. This approach will help you to gain an idea of how to bundle tasks and activities around each of the building blocks, in order to derive precise job descriptions.

The above considerations emphasize how important it is to investigate the business processes in order to ensure an efficiently performing operational management. It will quickly become clear to an investor that you run your company professionally. Moreover, if you were able to briefly present to him the most important business processes of your company and to convince him of a contemporary business, you would increase his willingness to invest into your company.

Your process map serves as basis for structuring your company. You can assess the main features of your organizational structure and shape them according to your business requirements.

5.2   Organizational structure

Based on the processes

- management processes,
- core processes and
- support processes

described in the last section, you can now generate the organizational structure and units. In order to simplify matters we have considered a company
with only one product and have avoided further differentiations and segmen-
tations. We will later point out the various organizational structures.

In accordance with the job descriptions, the tasks, the activities and the
responsibilities are assigned to the different organizational units. Depending on the volume and complexity of the different tasks, they will be assigned to one or more organizational units. Figure 5.3 shows the organizational structure according to the operational structure in chapter 5.1. This
approach is called a process-oriented organizational structure. In this particular example we have assigned each individual process to a specific

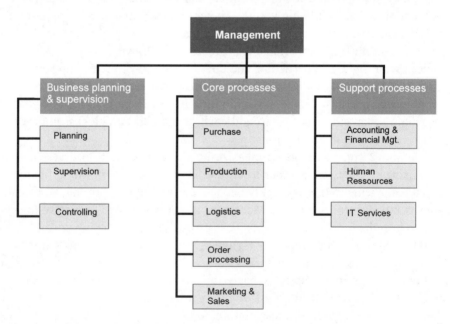

Fig. 5.3. A process-oriented organizational structure.

department within the three organizational units. The organizational units concentrate on the management board, where reporting paths converge.

You can summarise your organizational structure in an overall organization chart, where you will describe your different organizational units.

The design of the organizational structure allows you to focus on:

- either the essential processes – such as management, core and support processes – or
- the essential operational functions – such as procurement, development, production, marketing, administration – or
- the product lines respectively the customer target groups.

If you focus on the operational functions, a functional organization will be the result (fig. 5.4). If you focus on the product lines or customer target groups, a business unit or divisional organization will be the result (fig. 5.5).

In a functional organization (fig. 5.4) different products can be found in different functional areas, without there being a defined product management unit. The responsibilities are assigned from a functional point of view. In a divisional organization (fig. 5.5), however, the production, marketing, development and so forth are found in separate business units.

The choice of organizational form depends mainly on your product portfolio and the required sales channels and customer groups.

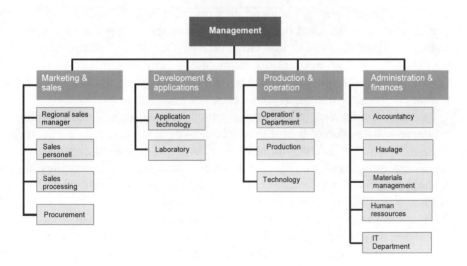

Fig. 5.4. Example of a functional organization.

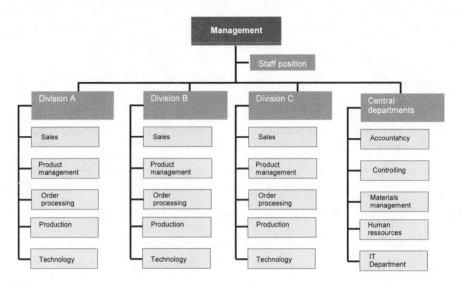

Fig. 5.5. Example of a divisional organization.

With a narrow homogeneous product programme for a homogeneous customer group, a functional organization is an excellent choice. Whether marketing is an own functional unit or part of the sales department or just a staff position, and whether controlling is a part of the administration or a staff position is of secondary importance and will depend on the competences and skills of your employees.

When a broad heterogeneous product program or a variety of customer groups exists, a divisional organization is preferable and promises greater market and customer proximity. However, for such an organizational form you should take into account that numerous fillings of similar functions, higher time consumption and resources for coordination usually result in higher personnel and infrastructure costs.

In many companies hybrid organizational forms have proved worthwhile, as you can derive from figure 5.6.

A company for instance might be designed as a divisional organization with separate distribution units, back offices, development and application technique groups, while sales, production, logistics and administration remain centrally organized. In this case the organizational linkage to the development department is to be considered very carefully because decentralization may result in parallel developments, if project and development plans are not appropriately synchronised. On the other hand, a central development department may have the disadvantage that priority will be given to the development of certain product lines or assortments and thus

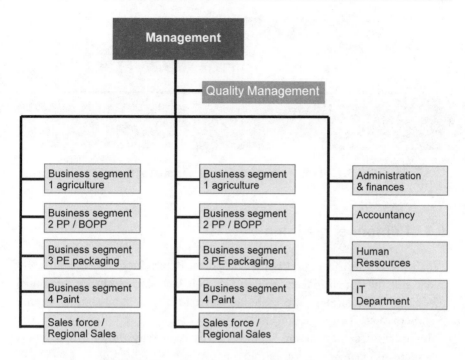

Fig. 5.6. Example of a hybrid organizational type.

will provide insufficient capacities for new business opportunities and the assortment of small target groups.

In a hybrid type of organization a careful coordination of the sales activities and customer accounts is necessary in order to prevent the concentration of different marketing units with different products on the same customer in order to make the buyer a competing offer.

Adapting organization is a crucial topic, particularly in high-growth companies, because these companies can often not fulfil existing requirements by means of the traditional type of organization. Increasing demand and product diversity as well as an expansion of the product assortment require an adaptation of the organizational processes and a restructuring of the functional areas for such companies. You should appropriately describe these modifications of your organizational structure in your business plan.

The organization structured according to fig 5.7 is run by two managers. It is a functionally oriented organization with a staff position for controlling which reports directly to the management. The areas of responsibility have been clearly structured and each has been filled by a defined person.

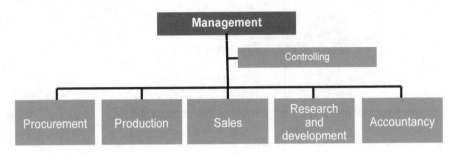

Fig. 5.7. Further example of an organizational structure.

5.3   Personnel planning

When the organizational structure has been determined and the different tasks and the functional areas defined, you can start with the personnel planning. Your strategy here should be to differentiate between regular members of staff and freelancers.

In order to achieve your business goals, you may either employ new members of staff or release employees. As an entrepreneur you will usually be confronted with a kind of natural fluctuation in the number of employees, taking into account retirements or resignations.

For the different functional areas, such as production, marketing and so forth personnel resources should be well-planned and scheduled. Be aware that a scarcity of personnel would affect your business as negatively as a surplus of personnel. Personnel scarcity would cause interruption of service and product delivery. In contrast a surplus of personnel would increase costs and inefficiency.

In order to give you an example, we have developed a personnel plan in accordance with the example in figure 5.7. The existing situation serves as a baseline for further planning of resources, dependent on the employees, the required operations and the transaction volumes.

Table 5.1 shows an example of personnel planning per functional area on a monthly basis, as well as the development of the number of employees including their payroll and social costs.

By means of personnel planning the personnel requirements can be determined, which are presented in job descriptions. The job descriptions of your employees should include the following essential elements:

Table 5.1. A personnel planning example.

	Month 1			...	Month 12			
	No. of Employees	Gross salary per Employee*	Personnel cost	...	No of Employees	Gross salary per Employee*	Personnel cost	Total
Management	2	13,0	26	...	2	14,3	29	328
Purchasing	13		47	...	16		61	650
Supervisor	1	7,0	7	...	1	7,4	7	86
Dept head	2	5,0	10	...	4	5,1	20	182
Clerks	10	3,0	30	...	11	3,1	34	382
Produktion	21		71	...	22		73	862
Supervisor	1	6,0	6	...	1	6,4	6	74
Technical	4	5,0	20	...	3	5,1	15	212
Clerks	16	2,5	40	...	18	2,6	46	515
Administration	2	2,5	5	...	2	2,6	5	61
Sales	38		172	...	48		231	2.419
Supervisor	2	8,0	16	...	2	8,6	17	199
Field sales	20	5,5	110	...	25	5,9	147	1.543
Sales support	6	3,5	21	...	10	3,7	37	351
Call-Center clerks	10	2,5	25	...	11	2,7	29	327
R & D	5		31	...	6		39	417
Supervisor	1	10,0	10	...	1	11,0	11	126
Technical	3	6,0	18	...	4	6,1	24	255
Assistant	1	3,0	3	...	1	3,1	3	36
Accounting	2		11	...	2		12	135
Supervisor	1	7,5	8	...	1	8,0	8	93
Accountant	1	3,5	4	...	1	3,6	4	43
Controlling	3		15	...	3		16	190
Supervisor	1	9,0	9	...	1	9,7	10	112
Controller	2	3,2	6	...	2	3,3	7	78
Total	84		373	...	99		460	5.001

- Name of job,
- Rank and name of the job holder,
- Aim of the job,
- Goals of the job holder,
- Tasks of the job holder,
- Demands on the job holder,
- Area of responsibility of the job holder and
- Its relationship to other jobs.

The job descriptions within your company should have a uniform structure. Since job descriptions frequently change, you should ensure that both their structure and content are continuously adapted and maintained.

5.4   Management team

As previously mentioned, your investors will expect description of your management team. You must explain which people will be responsible for the management of your company and what experience they have had in comparable positions in the past. Their educational and professional background will help to profile your management team.

Take into account that in the business world the most convincing criteria are real market success and customer satisfaction, both will ascertain sustainable revenue. However, technological knowledge and understanding can also be of significance if, for instance, you are active in a manufacturing area. Here, too, both the educational and professional background are significant. Furthermore, you should put emphasis on the business and financial skills of your management team: profound knowledge and professional experience in financial accounting, cost management, financing and controlling is essential.

However, market success, technological knowledge and business skills are only a minimum of criteria which should be fulfilled by your management team. In addition to this you should introduce the very individual and personal profile of your managers: their name, marital status, age, education, special merits and experiences etc. Keep in mind that the quality of your management team is the most critical success factor of your company.

Unfortunately, in practise, technological expertise often is well-profiled, yet a profound market expertise is missing. Hence, the professional reader will presume long term revenue and return on investment to be vulnerable. Check your management team to be sure whether you have established a balance between market, technology and finance orientation. This not only applies to start-ups but also to well-established companies.

Established companies should particularly check the follow-up regulations in their corporate management. A management team member's sudden exit can raise a considerable risk and endanger the survival of your company. You should clearly point out in your business plan how you intend to deal with this topic and whether you can already provide a solution.

5.5   Reporting systems

After having thus described your management team, you should attend to a description of your reporting system. In order to achieve highest transparency of your operational structure and the business processes within your organization as well as their related costs, you will be in the need of a qualified reporting system. Such a system would facilitate the overall transparency and managerial control over costs. A reporting system, however, not only provides an annual planning of your business and the resulting financial statements, but also a set of additional instruments:

- The structuring of the company towards cost centres, the planning of the related costs, the monthly recording of the accumulated costs per cost centre and the monthly accounting for cost transgressions by those responsible for the cost centres.

- A product or cost unit calculation with at least a six-monthly comparison between pre-calculation and post-calculation.

- A customer unit calculation at least with respect to corresponding profit margins and including the real marketing and sales costs.

- A monthly management report system in which the area managers describe the current course of market and costs and control deviations from the annual plan.

The following example demonstrates how a product can be presented by different types of analyses and differently interpreted throughout the reporting system. Figure 5.8 shows what information can be gained by different types of cost allocations.

When considering the costs of materials in contrast to margins, product line E appears to be the best. If costs of production and marketing (fig. 5.9) are assigned, then product lines A and B would contribute the same or even higher margins than product line E.

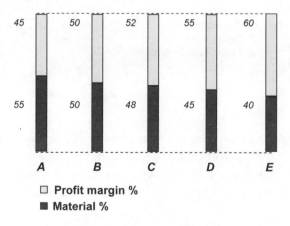

Fig. 5.8. Differentiation of product cost allocations.

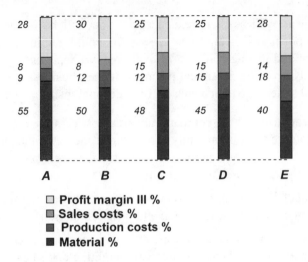

Fig. 5.9. Further differentiation of product cost allocations.

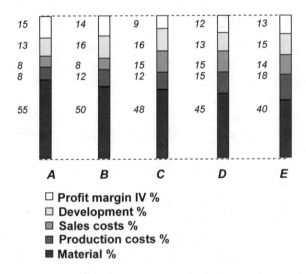

Fig. 5.10. Additional differentiation of product cost allocation.

The above example clearly shows the necessity of a refined reporting system and also shows that a profit and loss account would not even be sufficient on a monthly basis. You must be aware at an early stage which products will contribute to your profit margins and which products will not.

5.6 Legal form

Your investors will expect a concise description of the legal form of your company. When you start up a business, the right choice of legal form is crucial. Yet one should not forget that from an absolute business viewpoint the perfect legal form really does not exist. Every form has its strengths and weaknesses, advantages and disadvantages. The final choice depends upon:

- organizational laws,
- corporate laws,
- liability laws,
- tax laws and
- employment laws.

The choice via these criteria will have both personal as well as financial consequences for you yourself. You may for instance limit liabilities by choosing a limited liability corporate form. Unlike the founding of a business partnership, the limited liability corporate form is frequently associated with tax disadvantages. And if you attach importance to entrepreneurial independence, you may prefer to be sole proprietor.

A change of the legal form can be recommended, if you have been running a business for several years and topics such as succession regulations arise or new financing options are approached. For instance, if you have begun your business activity as a single entrepreneur and the company has grown to a critical size that makes a liability limit appear appropriate, the transition to a limited liability corporate form would be an option.

Keep in mind that the choice of the legal form of your company could have extreme economical and even existential consequences for your company as well as for you yourself. Therefore you should definitely consult both an experienced attorney and a tax accountant, before reaching any decision.

5.7 Key questions

- *How is the constellation of your management team planned?*
- *Are the demands of your business as addressed to the management team reflected in the qualifications, the skills and the experience of your managers?*

- *Are your managers offered regular internal or external training courses?*
- *Are further training courses subjects to contracts when employing managers?*
- *What is the average age of your management team?*
- *What are the tasks and responsibilities of your managers?*
- *What experience, knowledge, background education and professional references do your managers need?*
- *According to which criteria are your managers paid?*
- *Is incentive structure appropriate to that of your competitors?*
- *To what extent are performance targets set?*
- *How is the competence of your managers assessed?*
- *What about the continuity in the management team? Since when have the current managers been in their position?*
- *How often have the managers changed in the last 5 years?*
- *Are there certain succession regulations in the management?*
- *Who are the key persons in your management team?*
- *According to which standards and criteria were the members of your management chosen?*
- *With which organizational type can you realize your business model most successfully?*
- *With which organizational type (operational and structural) do you wish to achieve the best markets and customer proximity?*
- *Does your enterprise have some clear organization charts?*
- *To what extent is your organizational structure documented?*
  - *Organization chart*
  - *descriptions of function*
  - *determination of competence*
  - *internal controls*
- *How many hierarchy levels exist in your company (span of control)?*
- *How well is your company organization structured?*

- *Which are the main weaknesses of your organization?*

- *How do you plan to avoid time delays (through interfaces and unclear responsibilities), bottlenecks as well as duplications of work?*

- *How can you ensure quick reaction of your organization to sudden market changes?*

- *How do you achieve a flat organization and a fast flow of information?*

- *How do you ensure that responsibilities are delegated to the right person?*

- *To what extent does cross-sectional teamwork occur in your company?*

- *How do you ensure that the costs and profit responsibility corresponds to the products?*

- *Have you divided the company into cost sections?*

- *Have you considered the planning of the costs of the cost sections, and the monthly records of the accumulated costs per cost section?*

- *Have you considered the monthly arguments of the cost section representatives about costs transgressions?*

- *Do you provide a product profitability analysis or cost-unit accounting which allows at least a six-monthly balance between the pre-calculation and a post-calculation?*

- *Do you present a customer profitability calculation at least as a contribution margin accounting including the real marketing and sales costs?*

- *Which legal form does your company have?*

- *Have you considered the formalities, costs and possible publicity duties arising from your legal form?*

- *Do you want to restrict the liability, in the case of bankruptcy?*

- *Do you want to run your company as a single entrepreneur?*

- *Does it make sense to lower the risk and absorb additional know-how, by boarding new partners and shareholders?*

- *Do you wish to be the sole decision-making power?*

- *Have you already considered tax criteria?*

- *What influence does the legal form have on the image and profile of your company?*
- *Are there clear deputy arrangements?*
- *Has there been a change of the legal form, restricting liability in the last 2 years? If so, what change?*
- *What is the partnership and shareholder structure like? Who are the partners?*
- *What interest do your partners and shareholders have in further developing the company?*
- *Are there partners and shareholders with contrasting interests?*
- *Are there regulations limiting profit withdrawal?*
- *Are there regulations as to handing over shares to a third party?*
- *Do partners and shareholders perform management functions?*
- *What percentage of the joint capital is covered by the management itself?*
- *Do you have an advisory board?*
- *Who are the members of the advisory board?*
- *Which regulations exist for the designation of the advisory board?*
- *Is the advisory board competent enough to consult the management?*

6 Products and services

As soon as you have outlined your business idea roughly, you should have a critical look at your products and services – your added value carrier – for these form the basis of your business model. It is important that your products and services fit the needs of your customers: only if customers are prepared to pay a price for your products and services, is business done. Therefore it is necessary to describe the very unique features and characteristics of your products, the so-called unique selling propositions.

6.1 Product features

6.1.1 Unique selling propositions

Unique selling propositions are those features and characteristics which accentuate the uniqueness and excellence of your products on the market in order to be distinguished and preferred by the customers and to raise competitive advantages.

We have compiled some general aspects so that you can characterize the unique selling propositions of your products:

- The quality is discernibly higher than that of the competitors.
- The quality standard represented by the brand is maintained by constant product improvements and is never given up.
- The price is more favourable than that of the competitors while the quality is the same.
- The technological characteristics and features of your product are more advanced.
- The Design is more modern or satisfies the expectations of your customers much better than your competitors' do.
- The brand or the image of your product is more valuable.

- The construction and handling of the product are simpler.
- The development and production times are faster and confirmed delivery dates are kept.

6.1.2   Auxiliary services

Due to the high maturity of products on most markets and the high degree of similarity of the products within the markets, auxiliary services play an increasingly important role in distinguishing oneself from the competitors. For service companies in particular this differentiation is determined by the personal relationships of the company to its customers. With technical products it is also important to determine how well the product suits the customers' way of looking at a problem. At this point you should thoroughly consider and analyse your differentiation potential, which can decisively influence the price of the product and the satisfaction of the customers.

In order to help you characterize auxiliary services for your products, we have put together the following features:

- fast and flexible implementation of customisation
- better customer service and support,
- faster and more reliable supplying of spare parts,
- better complaint management,
- better customer relationship management,
- more regular and refined delivery of information,
- communication is guaranteed via modern media,
- customer friendly and diverse sales channels exist.

6.2   Product description

After determining the essential features and characteristics of your products, you should precisely describe your products and services. The descriptions of details in manufacturing and processing methods are not necessarily expedient, unless you can substantiate cost or quality advantages with them.

The specification of the benefits and advantages of your products and services are essential but often insufficient. Since customers usually buy products on the basis of their own specific needs, you should ask yourself, how your products suit your customers' needs: Which different technologies are applied to improve the products, how your technology will contribute to this, and in what periods of time future technological developments or changes in consumers' behaviour are to be expected etc.

Products which considerably resemble the products of your competitors are so-called me-too products. With such product copies you will only attain a lasting chance of long-term success, if you can either offer them at a more reasonable price or if you have been able to create serious entry barriers for your competitors throughout your product distribution net. Only then will customers feel encouraged to give up their brand loyalty. The advantage of a me-too strategy is the lowering of marketing costs, such as costs for market analysis and product design can be cut.

6.3   Product portfolio and product plan

As a rule a company offers more than only one product or service. The systematically composition of your services, products and their variants is called your product portfolio.

Both the analysis of an existing and the planning of a future product portfolio presuppose four essential steps:

- Identification of the relative market share (chapter 7) as well as the corresponding market growth. The relative market share determines your market position with respect to other competitors. The growth in percentage for each product indicates the general attractiveness of this type of product on the specific market.

- Description of the interrelations, interactions, mutual complementation and contrasts of your products both with respect to the exact product features and to your strategic objectives, product development, production, distribution, marketing, etc.

- Identification of all risks and opportunities which will occur through the combination and interaction of the products on different business and company levels. Also illuminate all risks and opportunities which may influence or compensate each other. A computer manufacturer, for instance, who attains high revenue rates by the sale of new computers in times of high market demand will cover himself in times of low demand through business with computer parts as well as service work.

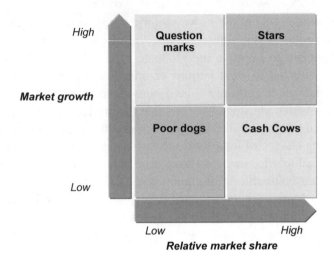

Fig. 6.1. Positioning of the products P1, P2 and P3 within a product portfolio.

- Distinction between:
  - less attractive products which, however, generate cash due to their high market share (cash cows),
  - attractive products which unfortunately generate less cash due a low market share (question marks),
  - less attractive products, that do not generate cash due to a low market share (poor dogs), and
  - attractive products which also generate cash due to their high market share (stars).

Among these four extremes, of course, there exist a great number of alternatives and options, as to how you can position your individual products within your product portfolio. Fig. 6.1 shows how you can present your product portfolio with regard to market attractiveness and market share in a typical portfolio chart.

As a result you may elaborate a compilation of all products which are planned to be discarded, extended, acquired or further applied for cash flow generation.

Based on the existing product portfolio and the product portfolio planned for the future, a roadmap can be developed which will describe the essential product features, the required activities, measures and resources for the transition from the existing portfolio to the target portfolio and which will assign them to a timeline.

6.4   Key questions

- *What are the special features and characteristics of your products?*
- *What are the unique selling propositions of your product?*
- *Which auxiliary services do you offer your customers?*
- *Which further unique selling propositions result from these auxiliary services for your products?*
- *Which advantages of your products and services back up your business?*
- *Which of your products is a me-too product?*
- *What are the strengths and weaknesses of your products and services?*
- *Which opportunities and risks will result from this in the future?*
- *Do you possess patents and trademarks? What is their period of validity?*
- *What running time do you give your present products?*
- *Which new products do you wish to introduce and within which period of time?*
- *Do you plan to substitute old products with new ones or to extend the market by introducing novel products?*
- *When will a product substitution take place?*
- *How do you organize your product assortment?*
- *According to which criteria do you prioritise your products?*
- *How is your product portfolio structured?*
- *What are the strengths and weaknesses of your portfolio?*
- *What are the resulting opportunities and risks for your business?*
- *Through which modifications of your product portfolio can you avoid future risks?*
- *Through which modifications of your product features, -variety and portfolio could you improve your future solvency?*
- *Taking into account all the above considerations, how would you design and develop an entire product plan?*

7 Market and competition

Your next challenge is to position your products and services on the market. In doing this you must be able to ascertain the attractiveness of both your current and future products on the market. You should furthermore convince the readers with profound understanding and knowledge that you can deal professionally with all those market forces which could have a lasting influence on your business.

Be aware that the market is not a virtual term, but a real force field of individual customers who want to purchase products and primarily fulfil their needs and wishes. Hence certain products compete with one another. Within your business plan you should consider both the market for your products as well as the character of your competitors. In this chapter we will focus on the main aspects of market and competition.

The results of your market and competition analysis will form the indispensable basis for the entire planning of sales and marketing, as will be discussed in chapter 8.

7.1 Market

7.1.1 Description of relevant market

With the description of your products and services (chapter 6), you have already provided a preliminary delimitation of your product market because your products are designed for certain target groups. The so-called relevant market consists of the target groups which are addressed by your products and services.

Furthermore, you must analyse how big your market is and what business potential you have at your disposal in the future. In order to assess the current market potential, take your revenues and sales volumes as a baseline, and from this starting point determine your current market volume and its course for the next budget years. Avoid the temptation to define your relevant market too broadly. Different customers have different product requirements and wish for different approaches. Describe as precisely as possible the clientele, that you do not want to approach by your regional, technological or marketing shot.

The information required for the determination of relevant markets could be obtained by external market research and intern investigations.

For consumer goods market the necessary data is raised by market research agencies e.g. via business and household panels. A panel is a selected, representative group of businesses or households whose sales and purchase records are evaluated regularly through systematic observations and surveys (primary research). However, on analysing data, it is recommended to fall back upon internal information sources, too, e.g. cost calculation documents, customer or general statistics and external information sources, such as publications by institutes, associations, national and international statistics offices or the press (secondary research).

Around markets for capital-intensive goods there are fewer translucencies. Here interviews with customers, upstream suppliers and also the manufacturers of the production machines can be very helpful, because they have a good insight into the investment behaviour of the competitors.

Of course, you almost always obtain the most significant information directly from your customers themselves:

- Why did your customers buy a certain product?
- How satisfied are your customers with the product?
- What do your customers like, what do they dislike?
- Would your customers buy the product again?
- At what price would your customers buy?
- How do your customers judge your company in comparison with your competitors?

In this case do not rely only on the statements of your sales and marketing departments. Talk with your customers and ex-customers yourself, too, but never forget that your customers are the captives of their own experiences and will rarely contribute valuable propositions for new products.

7.1.2 Market segmentation

Imagine the customer's problem was "the bonding of different materials". Bonding could be carried out by different techniques such as gluing, screwing, hot pressing, welding, riveting, pegging, stapling, nailing, etc. However, the applicability of a certain bonding technique depends on the properties of the material you want to bond. Hence, the various techniques and materials result in a large number of product-market-segments of different sizes and with a different potential for growth and profit.

This example shows how a market follows segmentation rules, which may not only be technological, but also dependent on price and quality.

Steigenberger, a family-owned German hotel group runs a precisely focused strategy within a very competitive market environment dominated by the big international hotels and their complex reservation systems. As a key measure the company in the course of time had developed four brands in order to attain market coverage at different price and quality levels. But in the autumn of *2003* the clock was turned back. Two brands were abandoned and the hotels were bundled into two brands, one at an exclusive level, "Steigenberger Hotels" and another in a lower price category, "Intercity Hotels".

Of course with regard to customer target groups you may distinguish by utilization aspects, local areas, market penetration, sales and distribution channels. End users can be further distinguished by their purchasing attitude, age-groups, income and fashion or brand preference. When applying segmentation, be sure not to fill too many segments with too many different products. The resulting complexity may overtax management capacity and exhaust the financial resources of the company.

The next example will show another type of market segmentation, applied by a manufacturer of optical products with five product lines:

- Torches,
- Binoculars and telescopic sights,
- Optical measurement systems,
- Projection lenses and
- Car lighting and sensory systems.

These product lines are suitable both for customers in industrial plants that process them and supply their own product and for the final customer who is reached via specialized trades. In the supply industry three customer groups are distinguished:

- Suppliers of car parts,
- Slide beamer manufacturers and
- Optical equipment manufacturing customers.

With respect to the direct end users, the company has focused on two retail targets:

- Hunting and sport trading shops on the one hand and

- Retailers and department stores for photographical and optical devices on the other.

The so-called *product-market-matrix* (fig. 7.1) exemplifies the market segmentation for the optical devices in Germany, where the dark fields show the customer groups for the individual product lines.

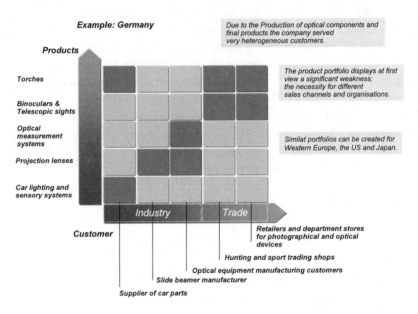

Fig. 7.1. Market segmentation for optical devices by means of the product-market-matrix.

If we take the product line of binoculars and telescopic sights, and characterize this product line according to price levels and application, as shown in figure 7.2. On the basis of the sophisticated price structure, one should consider which sales channel and which target audience one wishes to pursue in future? Is the target only the limited market of hunters reached via hunting and sport shops or is it the entire mass market for leisure pursuits reached via retailers and department stores?

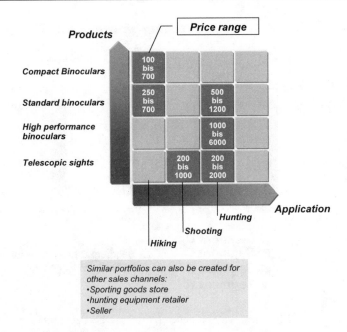

Fig. 7.2. Differentiation of the product line binoculars and telescopic sights with respect to price levels and application fields.

The above examples show, how you could conclusively represent your target markets and segments in your business plan.

7.1.3 Market growth

In order to be able to estimate your future business, it is necessary to investigate the growth of your market. You should quantify and estimate both revenue and sales volume for the next 3-5 years. In this case individual market segments could develop quite differently from the entire market itself. Market segments may for instance interact through mutual substitutions and in turn affect your sale potential negatively.

The example, shown in illustration 7.3, shows that the market segments D and B display a considerable market potential. Hence marketing and distribution should focus on these partial market segments.

Market growth is considerably influenced by trends and fashion, which can be social demographical, economical, technological as well as environmental. These trends can seriously affect the sales development of your products as well as the customer's consumer habits. One example of chang-

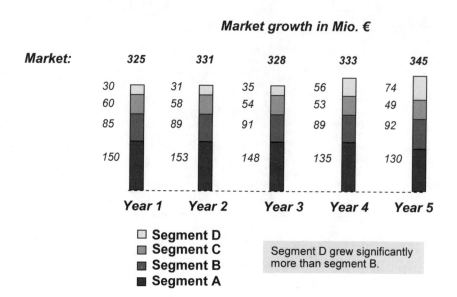

Fig. 7.3. The development of partial market segments.

ing consumer habits is the increasing health consciousness of the consumers in food industry. Customers increasingly prefer diet and low-fat products which are manufactured at higher rates due to the increasing demand.

7.2   Competition

When you have defined your market, you will become aware of the many competitors who are already active in the same market, thus putting all their efforts into winning the same target customers as you are. In order to win the battle, you need to develop successful market strategies. It is necessary to first determine the competitors and their market behaviour and tactics. In this case you should recognize whether these competitors are imitators, price breakers or innovators. Furthermore, you should realize how large the market share of your competitors is and understand the strategic advantages by which they have obtained their market shares. In particular you should identify who has priority in determining the key market rules (product leader, price leader, market size etc.). In the same way you should assess whether new competitors could penetrate your markets and thus influence market behaviour.

7.3 Market position

Your market position demonstrates your strength in the market and the outside business world. It is crucial to benchmark your market position in comparison with your competitors at any time (fig. 7.4). A market share of 25%, for instance, is not much, if there exists only one competitor who rules the market with a 75% share; on the other hand a market share of 25% represents a strong position, if there exist ten competitors and your top competitor has reached only a 12% share.

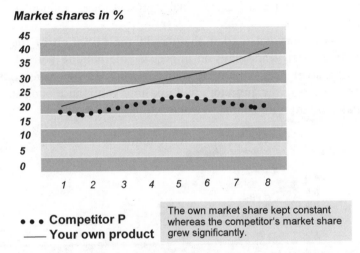

Fig. 7.4. Example of the development of market shares over seven years.

In order to determine your competitive strength on a specific market, the so called relative market share is applied:

$$RMS = \frac{\text{Own market share}}{\text{Market share of the main competitor}} \qquad \text{(Eq. 7.1)}$$

In terms of a quotient of the market shares, the relative market share indicates the gap between you and the main competitor on the market (tab. 7.1).

Table 7.1. The calculation of the relative market share.

Market share of the main competitor %	75	50	30	25	20	15	10
Own market share %	25	25	25	25	25	25	25
Relative market share %	0,33	0,50	0,80	1,00	1,25	1,66	2,50

According to table 7.1, if your market share is 25 % and the share of your main competitor 50 %, your relative market share will be:

$$RMS = \frac{25}{50} = 0,5$$ (Eq. 7.2)

However, if your main competitor obtains only 30 %, your relative market share will increase to 0,8; following this rule, if your main competitor obtains only 20 %, your relative market share will be about 1,25 and so forth.

Figure 7.5 shows an example of the development of the relative market share. In this way it is possible to compare the market positions of a company on the different markets and finally present these positions in a portfolio (chapter 6).

Next to your current market share itself the evolution of the market share over the last years plays an important role helping you to estimate the future market perspectives of your company. If you have constantly lost market shares your investors will ask how you plan to stop the negative trend and turn it into a positive one.

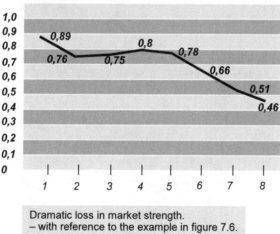

Relative market shares

Dramatic loss in market strength.
– with reference to the example in figure 7.6.

Fig. 7.5. Example of the relative market share.

7.4 Key questions

- *What is your target market?*
- *How is your target market segmented?*

- *Which problem solutions do you provide?*
- *What is your technological competence?*
- *Which market segments are relevant for your business?*
- *Which segments do you want to occupy?*
- *How big is your target market?*
- *What is the growth of your target market?*
- *What does the market growth depend on?*
- *What is your special competence in your market?*
- *What market position do you have?*
- *Has your market position worsened or improved during the last years?*
- *What are the mega-trends in your industry?*
- *Which new business opportunities do you envision?*
- *Which limitations may arise? Will legal regulations increase?*
- *Will demographic changes influence the markets?*
- *Which technological modifications may emerge?*
- *Who are your most important competitors?*
- *Which short- and long-term goals do your competitors pursue?*
- *How do your competitors view your company?*
- *Which competition strategies will you have to expect?*
- *Will your rivals tackle you or evade you?*
- *Which partial markets are especially significant for your main competitors, which ones are unimportant?*
- *In which fields of the business system are your competitors superior to you?*
- *Do your competitors produce at a more reasonable cost level?*
- *Do you have better access to raw materials?*
- *Do your competitors have more know-how in research and development?*
- *Are your rivals always a tic faster than you?*
- *Do your competitors react to market changes more quickly?*

- *Do your competitors use other sales channels?*

- *Do your rivals have close relationships to important customers?*

- *How competitive is your market?*

- *Do your rivals deal according to the motto "live and let live – there is room for all of us", or do they practice a hard crowding-out?*

- *Have old competitors already given up? Are there newcomers? Are there others, still standing at the door?*

- *Will the competition intensify in the future?*

- *How do your customers judge your enterprise in comparison with your competitors?*

- *Who are the customers for the products? Have you described the main customer groups and changes to be expected?*

- *Who are the target customers of your business?*

- *Which part of the customer potential do you want to cover in the future?*

- *Why did the customers buy a certain product from your portfolio?*

- *How satisfied are the customers with the product?*

- *What do the customers like, what do they avoid?*

- *Would the customers buy it again?*

- *At which price would the customers buy?*

- *Did you lose any important customers last year? For what reasons?*

8   Marketing and sales

In chapter 7 we have described the basic conditions for your business model. Therewith you now know your target groups or customers, your market volume, market trends as well as your immediate competitors. In this chapter you will deal with the question with which marketing strategy and marketing concept you will be able to achieve your strategic goals.

8.1   Marketing

8.1.1   Marketing strategy

Your marketing strategy describes your market objective and marketing goals for the next years. Furthermore, it should determine the market share which you wish to achieve in your target market with your particular product portfolio, as well as the average market growth. You will have to plan your advertising and marketing costs accordingly.

When formulating your marketing strategy you should consider carefully which pricing you wish to embark on your customers (section 8.1.3).

From the individual market segments you can derive segment specific strategies. Thereby e.g. industrial customers, commercial customers or end users are treated differently, according to the following criteria:

- Advertising and marketing media
- Services and auxiliary services
- Competitive orientation
- Customer profitability
- Customer loyalty
- Acquisition of new customers.

Based on your marketing strategy the operative measures are derivated and provided with appropriate budgets. This is the subject of the marketing plan which represents one of the most crucial management tools.

8.1.2   Marketing plan

The business plan should include at least a three-year marketing plan, which sums up the sales targets for each product and product line (1 to …), explains the core marketing measures (tab. 8.1) and their risks and which also contains a timeline of planned product launches as well as a reasonable allocation of marketing costs.

The marketing plan thus represents a roadmap of the marketing activities which are necessary in order to achieve the strategic marketing goals.

Table 8.1. Sample roadmap for sales activities.

Measures /activities	Date		Responsible
Activity	Start	End	
Sales campaign for product 1 - direct marketing			
Sales campaign for product 1 - E-Mail			
E-Mail campaign for the accessory of product 1			
Telephone campaign for the accessory of product 1			
Event for product 2			
E-Mail campaign for product 3			
E-Mail campaign for the accessory of product 1			
E-Mail campaign for product 2			

The marketing plan should above that also include the development of your market share with regard to your competitors as well as the analysis of main market trends.

Table 8.2 shows a sample data sheet for the collection of the marketing plan's key data. The data are listed product-related or product line-related and span the last *2* years as well as *3* plan years.

8.1.3   Pricing policy

A key to the success of your business is the appropriate pricing policy. Every investor will ask you, according to which criteria you arrange your prices. If your prices are too high, you will not be able to attract customers and expect orders within your competitive environment. If your prices are too low, you will risk steering your company into the loss area. You will only be able to answer the question about the optimal price, if you, on the one hand, dispose of an internal controlling and cost input system and if you, on the other hand, regularly observe your competitors, their pricing policies and the price elasticity of the market.

Table 8.2. The main records required for the marketing plan.

	LY*	CY*	PY* 1	PY* 2	PY* 3
Product / product group 1					
Market share (%)					
Market volume (€)					
Percentage of sales [%]					
Sales Volume (quantity)					
Revenue (€)					
Marketing costs (€)					
Advertising costs (€)					
Product performance (€)					
Product / product group...					
Market share (%)					
Market volume (€)					
Percentage of sales [%]					
Sales Volume (quantity)					
Revenue (€)					
Marketing costs (€)					
Advertising costs (€)					
Product performance (€)					
Total					
Total marketing costs (€)					
Total advertising costs (€)					
Overall result (€)					

* LY: Previous year; CY: Current year; PY: Plan year

According to our observations many middle class companies have defined their prices corresponding to an overhead calculation and "bottom up": Surcharges for general expenses and for business profits were slammed on the (often inaccurately) calculated production costs. The adding up then results in the market price, whereupon sales department could give deductions – often without being informed about the marginal costs.

A completely different approach is the target cost plan. Before every development of a new product it is checked by market research with which price the biggest prospects of market success exist in a specific competitive environment. Based on these findings a price is defined. From this the cost structure is derived "top down": the required profit, the amount of required general expenses, and the residual amount for production.

A successful approach for a price alignment exists therein that you observe your own price deviations from the market average continually and assess which changes of the market share are due to price modifications (fig. 8.1).

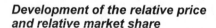

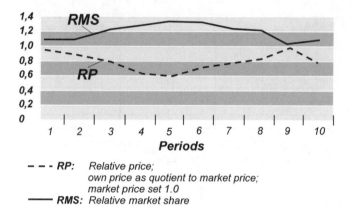

Fig. 8.1. The courses of relative price and relative market share.

The central questions for the evaluation of your pricing policy are:

- How are the prices determined for the individual products and who is responsible for that?

- Which information about material and production costs, product specific development and marketing costs, prices of the competitors, the price flexibility of the market flow into the price quote or price fixing?

- How do you detect the prices of the competitors?

- Are there references to price agreements?

- What is the extent to which sales and marketing is allowed to discount?

- Who is allowed to enter price variations into your system?

- Which cost information system do you use for pricing? Are post-calculations carried out regularly?

- Can you record and allocate product-related additional costs, which develop from rejects, additional material use, repair services, warranty services and service costs?

- How did market prices develop? Which future price developments can be expected?

- How far can cost increases be passed on to customers?

8.1.4   Advertising and sales promotion

The significance and the kind of advertising and sales promotion vary strongly among markets.

It has to be carried out a planning of advertising for consumer goods, that are bought regularly (e.g. foods and toiletries), for over-the-counter-drugs and for durable consumer goods. The/This plan has to include the main advertising message and budget, the selection of advertising media (television, journals, daily papers and so forth) as well as possible cooperation with advertising, sales promotion and public relation agencies. The selection and suitability of advertising media are mainly determined by the advertising goals as well as by geographical, quantitative and qualitative access to the target customers (generations, income levels, residence etc.).

The annual media analysis helps by displaying the audiovisual habits and literacy as well as the media coverage.

Sales promotion in the field of consumer business should be planned extremely carefully, in order to ensure their acceptance with the retailers, as well as their sales potential and success.

In mid-size companies, that do not produce a branded product for the final consumer, but semi finished, preliminary products or components for other companies, advertising and sales promotion are mainly restricted to brochures, fairs and public relation campaigns.

8.1.5   Marketing organization

Marketing objectives are usually regarded as top priority. Thus either the entrepreneur himself or the marketing manager will take care of them. If marketing exists as an organizational unit, it often concerns a staff unit for producing brochures, organizing sales promotion and managing fairs. Duties and responsibilities which are perceived by product managers are not carried out in these staff units.

If the company provides several product lines for different target groups, it is wise to establish an independent product management.

The responsibilities of the product management are product planning (section 6.3), the internal coordination of the company's product-related activities, market research and the cooperation with external service providers as advertising and market research agencies as well as package designers. The organization and updating of the internet representation also is to be addressed to the marketing organization.

8.2 Sales

8.2.1 Sales strategy

The sales strategy is based on the marketing strategy and turns it into operative sales objectives. You should consider the following questions with respect to the sales strategy:

- Which customers should be contacted in what frequency?
- Which key customers should you pay special attention to?
- Have you analysed the causes of customer loss? Which conclusions have you derived from this?
- Do you serve the right customers, those customers possessing the highest growth potential?
- Which potential prospects are supposed to be won? Especially in trade: How should distribution be expanded?
- Which market objectives are defined for the individual customers?
- Which profit margin goals are defined for the individual customers?
- With which organizational type do you wish to approach the market?

The implementation of the sales strategy in the sales goals allows the development of the sales organization and the corresponding processes. On the one hand within the framework of a sales plan, you should describe your current situation, on the other hand does it outline a roadmap which helps you achieve your future goals and objectives. In the following we will discuss the basic issues of a sales organization and the basic elements of a sales plan.

8.2.2 Sales organization

As an entrepreneur you have to decide, how you wish to approach the market, whether to build up your own sales team or for example work with sales representatives. The choice of the optimal sales method depends on the customers as well as on your relationship with them. A good relationship is needed for successful business.

If the number of your customers is restricted, if for instance you are a subcontractor in the automobile industry and only supply half a dozen of companies, you would need a small, but highly productive sales team for

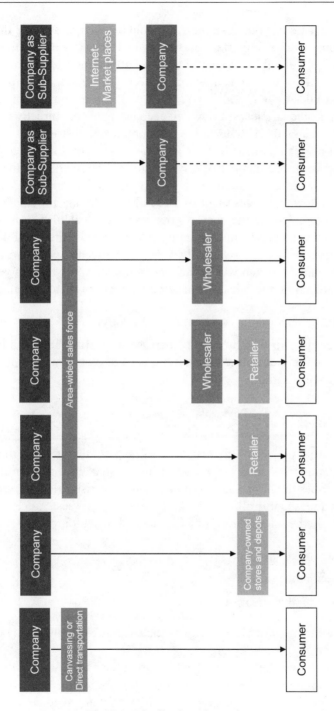

Fig. 8.2. Distribution channels.

the intense care of your customers. It could be even reasonable that you as a CEO take care of important customers yourself. If you sell to end users via trade, you should make up your mind about the size of your sales organization. The question is how many shops you aim at, if you only supply the wholesaler or not, and if you want to focus on franchisors and only serve the headquarters with few key account managers directly. Figure 8.2 shows the many alternatives of the sales organization structure.

If you need an area-wide sales approach, the size of the sales organization depends on the number of sales personnel, the retail area, the sales objectives and the cost structure of your products. For instance, if the cost structure allows an investment of *10%* of the revenue for sales activities, you have to calculate the size of your team. The calculation involves the capacity of the sales team as regards customer calls, the possible number of customer visits per day, and the required frequency per year. Important customers are contacted weekly, others monthly or only twice a year.

When planning the sales organization payment plays a crucial role:

- How is the variable compensation structured?
- According to which criteria (increase of profit margins, turnover increase, new customer acquisition, etc.) do you plan the variable part of compensation?

8.2.3 Sales plan

The business plan should include a sales plan for at least three years, which summarises sales targets according to markets and customers (1 to ...), describes the basic sales activities with their risks along a timeline and contains a reasonable allocation of distribution expenses.

Basically the sales plan should capture following topics:

- planning of the sales,
- planning the customers and
- planning the sales area.

The customer plan (table 8.4) covers the customer-oriented sale budget and corresponds to the sales plan.

After defining the markets, the question arises of how you aim to characterize, structure and evaluate your customers within the different markets. Depending on the geographic position of your customers, you should

Table 8.3. Sample sheet for sales records.

	LY*	CY*	PY* 1	PY* 2	PY* 3
Product / product group 1					
Sales Volume					
Unit price (€)					
Gross sales [%]					
Revenue reduction (€)					
Other distribution costs (€)					
Net sales (€)					
Product / product group...					
Sales Volume					
Unit price (€)					
Gross sales [%]					
Revenue reduction (€)					
Other distribution costs (€)					
Net sales (€)					
Total					
Sales Volume					
Unit price (€)					
Gross sales [%]					
Revenue reduction (€)					
Other distribution costs (€)					
Net sales (€)					

* LY: Previous year; CY: Current year; PY: Plan year

Table 8.4. Customer plan.

	LY*	CY*	PY* 1	PY* 2	PY* 3
Customer / customer group 1					
Sales Volume					
Unit price (€)					
Gross sales [%]					
Revenue reduction (€)					
Other distribution costs (€)					
Net sales (€)					
Customer / customer group...					
Sales Volume					
Unit price (€)					
Gross sales [%]					
Revenue reduction (€)					
Other distribution costs (€)					
Net sales (€)					
Total					
Sales Volume					
Unit price (€)					
Gross sales [%]					
Revenue reduction (€)					
Other distribution costs (€)					
Net sales (€)					

* LY: Previous year; CY: Current year; PY: Plan year

finally decide whether to develop the customer plans per field or not. This approach will affect the raising of a sales area plan.

Along the preparation of the sales plan you should ascertain that it corresponds to your marketing plan. The data base and structure as well as the roadmaps developed for both marketing and sales have to be adjusted to each other. This requires excellent communication of both the marketing and the sales project team during the business plan project.

8.3   Key questions

- *Which marketing actions have you defined?*
- *Which performance bond do you promise your customers by the use of your means of communication?*
- *What communication and advertising strategy do you have?*
- *Which advertising media do you use?*
- *What advertising expenditures do you plan?*
- *What degree of advertising impact do you reach in comparison to your competitors?*
- *How do you organize your marketing department?*
- *Who is responsible for marketing?*
- *Who defines the marketing budget?*
- *Do you require a team for your marketing?*
- *To what extent do you practice marketing within your company?*
- *To what extent do you cooperate with public relation agencies?*
- *Do you outsource sales and marketing partly or completely?*
- *Who controls marketing activities and budgeting?*
- *With which price strategy do you offer your products?*
- *Who determines the prices for your products?*
- *Does a pricing policy exist in your company?*
- *How do you ensure frequent price comparisons?*
- *What is your distribution strategy?*
- *Have you documented a distribution strategy?*

- *Which sales channels do you use and which ones could be still opened up?*
- *Are your products distributed via internet or via franchising?*
- *Does a structured sales organization exist?*
- *How does the geographical setting of the field work look like?*
- *How do office work and field work cooperate?*
- *How do you pay the sales representatives (fixed salary, bonus, incentives, etc.)?*

9 Research and development

The future business potential of your company is mainly based on your innovations and development projects. Therefore you should carefully present your research and development competences and your plans for new products and services in your business plan.

9.1 Presentation of research and development

Product design can only be successful if, on the one hand, one gets precise information about customer preferences and needs through marketing and if, on the other hand, the products are developed in close cooperation with the manufacturing department. Furthermore, marketing information is required about:

- the mega-trends of the markets,
- the achievable prices on the market and
- the required product differentiation for the different target groups

as well as an early cooperation with the purchasing department. The relationships between the research and development department and other areas of the value chain are shown in figure 9.1.

Base the description of your research and development strategy on the information from neighbouring areas like marketing, production and purchasing; hereby answer the following questions:

- Do you have the required competence within your company?
- Do you frequently buy research and development activities?
- Have you entered into a strategic alliance with other companies as regards the distribution of development tasks according to construction groups or fields of technology?

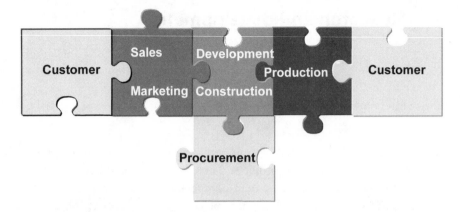

Fig. 9.1. The relationships of the research and development department with other areas of the value chain.

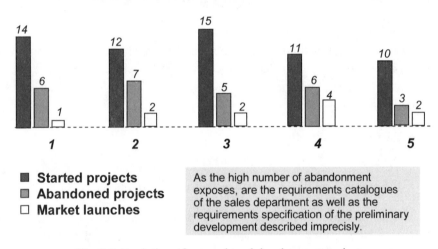

Started projects
Abandoned projects
Market launches

As the high number of abandonment exposes, are the requirements catalogues of the sales department as well as the requirements specification of the preliminary development described imprecisly.

Fig. 9.2. Evolution of research and development projects.

Show that your company's development is on an equal level to that of your competitors and convince your investors that you have taken measures in order to maintain this position in the future.

The factors that incur rising costs in development are nonexistent or insufficient project management, time and cost control, capacity planning.

The efficiency of your research and development department can be checked by different questions:

- How often has development been abandoned with reference to the number of started projects, compared to accomplished projects (fig. 9.2)?

- How high is the capacity of development when one compares the offers made and the orders received?

The assessment of your competitiveness should be shown in a so- called research and development portfolio. Figure 9.3 shows an example of such a portfolio, where research and development expenditure was regarded versus the number of annual new project introductions.

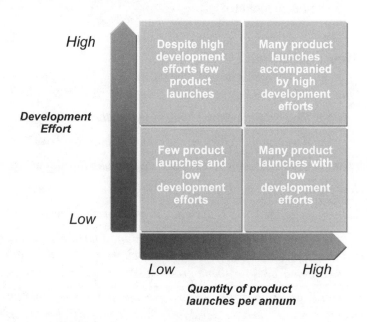

Fig. 9.3. The research and development portfolio.

Table 9.1. The essential core data for planning development.

Information	LY*	CY*	PY*		
			1	2	3
Personell costs (€)					
External costs (€)					
Employees (number)					
Project ongoing (number)					
Employee utilization (days)					
Abandoned projects (number)					
Market launches (number)					
Total costs for development (€)					

* LY: Previous year; CY: Current year; PY: Plan year

9.2   Development plan

The business plan should include at least a three-year research and development plan that summarises the main research and development objectives, the main development projects and measures, as well as the related activities and risks (Tab. 9.1). In addition to this, a time schedule for the planned launching of production and a wise distribution of the development costs should be included.

9.3   Key questions

- *What are your entire development costs with respect to sales?*
- *How has the cost allocation changed within the last 3-5 years?*
- *Are your development costs on the common industry level?*
- *What are your personnel costs for research and development?*
- *How many staff is employed in research and development?*
- *What share of the costs is assigned to outsourced services?*
- *How are your development costs distributed through basic research and development, new products, care, changes, adaptation constructions and measures for the upgrade of your current assortment?*
- *Do you develop your product programme along your company's own strategic goals, do you develop on the behalf of clients, or do you mainly acquire patents and licenses?*
- *Which role do marketing and sales play in the initiation of new projects?*
- *Do you have (if you work internationally) several competence centres for different products or technologies? How do you ensure the transfer of knowledge in this case?*
- *Are you a market leader with your research and development know-how, are you average with your technological knowledge, or are you an imitator?*
- *How do you observe technological mega-trends?*
- *How far are your current technologies endangered by possible substitution?*

- *Do you have at your disposal a project management for research and development that can show the current status of the project and its costs?*

- *What is the development success rate? What is the abandonment rate?*

- *How long is the average development time until the first production in series begins?*

- *Does your controlling system enable you to consider development changes demanded by your customers? Does it also enable you to calculate the increased development costs associated with that?*

- *Are you faster or slower with your research and development offers than your competitors?*

- *How efficient is the coordination of research and development with the marketing, production and purchasing departments? Are the purchasing and production departments   involved at an early stage?*

- *Does the development department regularly receive information from the production department about tool-related and material-related manufacturing problems, rejects rates and defects?*

- *Have you protected important technologies and procedures through patents or registered designs?*

- *How do you control whether competitors breach your patent or registered design protection?*

- *Are you yourself a licensee of the procedures or product components which are essential for the success of your business?*

- *Are there problems related to your licenses, for instance term limits?*

- *Have you formulated a research and development strategy for your enterprise? Have you coordinated it with your marketing, sales and production goals?*

10 Production

10.1 Outline of production

In this chapter you show your investors that your production operates smoothly and without greater problems. Hereby you show that your production is able to compete with others in regard to delivery times, reliability and production costs. You should particularly pay attention to the following points:

- the production volume, your own share in production and that done by outsourcing
- the production locations,
- the quality strategy,
- the status quo of the manufacturing technology,
- the investment requirement,
- the workflow in handling orders with the help of logistics and
- the qualifications of the employees.

Explain to your investors which manufacturing steps and added value stages your production process consists of, for instance prefabrication, component manufacturing, assembly, packing and which ones are carried out by subcontractors. Here you should also consider the manufacturing method, i.e. single-part production, brand, serial or mass production. In this context it is important to mention which production stages are given to external companies (outsourcing).

Outsourcing, however, only then makes sense if the external costs, which always include the overheads and surplus charges, are lower than your own actual full cost for the examined internal area. Furthermore, you should take the quality of subcontractors into consideration, as well as the extent to which they are controllable, responsive and flexible. Among other things, you should ask yourself the following questions:

- Does the external marketing organization accept that the services granted will differ according to the products, the customer groups and the regions?

- What delays will have to be taken into account with an outsourcing company?

The following examples should make the case clearer:

- Small pharmaceutical companies prefer outsourcing the production of certain galenic forms (tablets, pills, drops, ointments, suppositories) to specialists.

- Industries processing metal and plastics prefer to outsource coating and assembly work with high manual expenditure to countries with low wages and labour costs.

By means of the lead times for an order you can establish the required machine capacity for a certain period of time. If your planned capacity differs from the real one, additional costs (idle time costs) will arise due to under-utilized machines, whereas over-utilized machines will cause a production bottleneck. This will result in your having to buy external services and work overtime in production.

Describe the technological status quo of the utilization and workload of your plants and machines in the manufacturing processes. Answer the following questions:

- What is the utilization of the machine capacity like?

- Do you have bottleneck machines?

- Are capacity enlargements required?

- Are your rejects rates lower or higher than those of the competitors? What are the reasons for that?

- Also describe your quality strategy:

- What quality standard have you achieved in comparison with your competitors?

- Is there a quality management system in your company?

- What standards do you wish to achieve?

If you want to assess your quality strategy, you should analyse the entire costs that are associated with it. They include not only the costs of quality

control, but also the expenditure for blunders, to which the following cost
groups belong: rejects, finishing, additional deliveries, guarantees, commercial and technical fairness.

10.2 Production plan

The business plan should include at least a three-year production plan
which summarises the production strategy and contains a wise distribution
of the production costs. It should show the relevant risks and the planned
investments, and it should describe the essential measures for an increase
in performance (tab. 10.1).

Table 10.1. Sample sheet for the records of production planning.

Information	LY*	CY*	PY*		
			1	2	3
Production volume (quantity)					
Utilization of the capacity (%)					
Employees (number)					
Costs of material (€)					
External services (€)					
Personell costs (€)					
Depriciation (€)					
Other production costs (€)					
Total quality costs (€)					
Total production costs (€)					
Production costs / revenue (%)					

* LY: Previous year; CY: Current year; PY: Plan year

10.3 Key questions

- *How high are your entire production costs compared to your turnover, in per cent?*

- *How has the percentage changed in the last 3-5 years?*

- *What is the contribution of external services (raw material and purchased parts)?*

- *How high are your personnel costs in manufacturing?*

- *How many employees are occupied in manufacturing? How many
  machine operators and how many managers?*

- *Do you yourself manufacture your complete product programme, or do you get parts of the finished goods from other manufacturers?*

- *Do you manufacture in one location or at several locations? Do you assemble at the customers' locations or on construction sites?*

- *Do you provide made-to-order or made-to-stock manufacturing alternatives for producing series or limited lots?*

- *What modifications do you wish to carry out with regard to the vertical range as well as location of manufacturing within the next years?*

- *What is your main manufacturing bottleneck? Product lines, individual machines, machine capacity, process control, quality of instruments and tools, qualifications of the employees?*

- *Do the demand and the weekly output strongly vary through seasonal influences?*

- *Who is responsible for cost control of the finished goods warehouse? The marketing department, the production or an independent logistics?*

- *Are you competitive with respect to your production costs? Do you produce more or less cheaply than your main competitors do?*

- *Do you have production cost disadvantages in contrast to your rivals because of lower capacity, worse machines or technology, unfavourable basic conditions (personnel, organization, and plant layout) or because of more manifold versions and smaller lot sizes?*

- *Who determines the lot sizes? Production or marketing?*

- *With respect to your material suppliers, are you dependent on few providers or the strict directives of your customers?*

- *Do your upstream suppliers deliver in time and without errors? Do you have just-in-time arrangements with subcontractors?*

- *Do quality problems arise with respect to bad precursory material, inadequate product design, inappropriate process control, out-of-date machines or organizational weaknesses?*

- *Do you keep to the delivery times promised to your customers or do manufacturing delays occur?*

- *Do you tackle quality problems and manufacturing delays on time?*

- *How high is the number of completed deliveries compared to the total number of deliveries in per cent?*

- *How high is the number of customer complaints and returns compared to the total number of deliveries in per cent?*

- *How high are your guarantee costs compared to your total revenue in per cent?*

- *How high are your total quality costs (estimated) compared to your total revenue in per cent?*

- *Do you have a management information system which determines the essential parameters of production on time?*

- *What is the average lead time for a customer order (from the day of order confirmation up to delivery) in days?*

- *What is the frequency of your raw material turnover?*

- *What is the frequency of the finished product turnover?*

- *Do you pay by piecework rates, wage bonus or by hourly wage?*

- *How high are your maintenance and repair costs? How high is the share of outsourced services?*

- *How high are your annual investments in machines and manufacturing processes?*

- *Are you on an average level of investment in your industry, or are you on a lower or higher level?*

- *Are you investing in standard technologies, in process changes or in the introduction of completely new technologies this year?*

- *Do you know the status quo of the manufacturing technology of your main competitors?*

- *Have you carried out any larger projects to reduce manufacturing costs in the last three years? Were you successful?*

- *Are you planning any further rationalization projects for this year and for the near future? What are your goals?*

- *Have you formulated a manufacturing strategy for your company and coordinated this with your sales and development goals and strategies?*

11 Procurement and logistics

In your business plan you should briefly show that you are competitive in managing those operations that support production. The success of a good product must not fail because the purchasing department gives away potentials or because unnecessary costs and competitive disadvantages are caused by delays along the supply chain and logistics.

11.1 Purchase

There exists a general tendency of pushing added value towards outsourcing. Although in the majority of companies this tendency causes the share of material costs and external services to increase, purchasing departments are still largely operating as traditional mid-size order departments and not as modern procurement management units. The potential of optimizing the purchasing system and hence improving the profit margins is often neglected. In many companies it is precisely in procurement via the internet that there is still quite a great deal of potential.

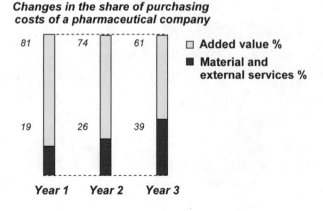

Fig. 11.1. Changes in the share of purchasing costs.

A key to success in purchasing is focusing on few but excellent suppliers. Since this aspect has been discussed for years companies are already well advanced in this respect and many procure up to 80 percent of their purchasing volume from less than 20 percent of their suppliers. The really efficient purchasers have advanced this even further and, following the Japanese example, have been able to reduce purchasing costs by concentrating 80 percent of their purchasing volume on less than 10 percent of their suppliers. This concentration not only simplifies the time required for managing the link to the supplier, it also strengthens the intensity of the company's relationship to key suppliers.

Many issues that are relevant to procurement can only be optimized by a cross-over approach if there is cooperation between the different departments, research and development, logistics, production, sales and marketing.

Below we will show a cross-functional optimization, taking the machine building industry branch as an example.

The Lindentaler machine building plant produces printing presses. First the company brought the small model M10, then the big model M90 onto the market. The basic version of M10 prints with 4 colours, M90 prints with 8 colours and larger formats. Since the market was focused on a mid size format, the company introduced the model M40 which achieved the performance of the larger M90 for mid-size formats (fig. 11.2).

On doing final costing of delivered M40 machines it turned out that all the machines caused losses. In a common analysis of development, purchase *and production costs a comparative value analysis of the different product lines was carried out. The analysis showed that the construction of several components of the M40 had been too expensive, and partly exceeded the costs of the M90.*

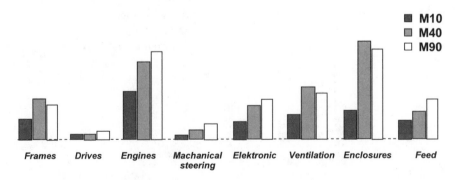

Fig. 11.2. Value analysis of the machine parts.

As a result of this, constructions were changed while at the same time the procurement department was searching for new suppliers and the workflows in production were being optimized. The common efforts resulted in cost savings of about 23 % (fig. 11.3).

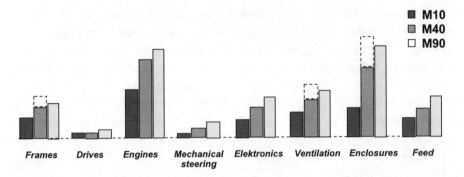

Fig. 11.3. Cost savings for the product line M40.

Next to concentrating on the main suppliers and using the internet market places, the use of key figures to steer procurement helps to save purchase costs. In order to simplify the process of dealing with internal orders, large companies started years ago to enable their employees to order non-production related materials via intranet catalogues. The purchasers now only pay attention to the catalogue offers and try to obtain the procurement goods offered there at the most reasonable price possible.

You should draw up your purchasing and procurement plan basing it on your purchasing strategy and the organization of your purchasing department. Show your investors that you have recognized the signs of the times and that you have at your disposal an efficient purchasing department which does not haggle over annual price cuts in the traditional customer-supplier-relationship, but is involved in the process of developing new products.

11.2 Logistics

In order to be able to judge the efficiency of your flow of materials, it is necessary to describe whether you manufacture made-to-order or make-to-stock. Afterwards you should plan your material requirements. In order to have minimum stocks on hand at maximum disposition, a material requirements planning has to be carried out.

The stock analysis, which is possibly based on specific operation scheduling and production planning systems, has to be taken into consideration, too. With make-to-stock manufacturing for instance you should determine in your business plan the stock turnover, the stock interest and the development of these values in the last years.

If in the course of years more and more new products or product variants are included in the assortment and the assortment volume increases, the question of clearing the assortment and reducing the variants arises within the entire planning framework. As a rule, such a clearing process leads to cost reductions and an increase in profitability. The reduction of the assortment should, however, be planned very carefully, for it can often lead to target conflicts between sales, production and logistics: Sales, for instance, is not usually interested in a small assortment; big assortments, however, are not economical as a rule and cause considerable costs, among other things logistics:

- storage volume,
- repository value,
- storage area and facilities, as well as
- storage management expenditures.

Procurement and storage planning must guarantee the necessary flexibility – through central storage, special sizes or specific arrangements with the suppliers.

A careful planning of the storage stages and the field warehouses enables you to keep the stock volume as low as possible. In this case one can aim at reducing the warehouse stages directly or optimizing the disposition per stage. A company that holds a large number of regional and decentralized warehouses, due to the high haulage and its strategic goal of short-term supply to customers, can often simply reduce its overall inventory by introducing specific and optimized disposition and supply rules for the field warehouses.

Remember that the optimal lot size or rather order quantity is directly proportional to the stock volume – a safety margin included. Hence one should carry out the calculation, planning and optimization of the lot sizes carefully when dealing with expensive articles of high stock value. Ordering and storage costs are needed to calculate the lot sizes. Storage costs consist of:

- costs of capital investment lockup and interest,

- the storage costs such as depreciation, insurance, taxes etc.,

- the space and area costs,

- the extra costs for special storage such as cold storage or the storage of dangerous items,

- the imputed interest for storage facilities etc.,

- the personnel costs as well as

- the maintenance and operating costs.

When planning the lot sizes and stock quantities you should also consider possible discounts as well as price increases.

For the optimal planning of the entire logistics, the most essential factors influencing performance are the choice and number of locations. When choosing a location you should consider the following cost factors:

- the delivery costs,

- the storage costs,

- the production costs,

- the transport and distribution costs as well as

- the possible revenues, resulting from direct sales.

The influence of research, development and construction activities on the logistics costs is often underestimated. When planning research and development you should pay attention to:

- the variety of parts is kept as small as possible (for instance through intelligent unit construction systems),

- the range of products is kept as small as possible (for instance through rigorous standardization of the products, finished parts, semi-finished products or raw materials),

- manufacturing and derivation of the product variants is moved as far as possible to the end of the value chain and

- how products are designed and constructed so as to justice waste management (for instance by avoiding materials that would cause ecological damage and by using recycling).

With regard to transport and turnover you should pay attention to a number of rules of thumb when planning and adopting the flow of materials, namely:

- to avoid internal and external transport as far as possible,
- to shorten transport paths as far as possible,
- to extend transportation intervals as far as possible,
- to reduce the number of turnover and delivery locations as far as possible,
- to rationalize the loading and unloading process and,
- provided it is useful and cost saving, to automate transportation.

The internal haulage should also be considered when planning the logistics. When doing this, determine:

- the most effective transportation requirements and the corresponding quantity structure and
- the actual costs of the sections as well as of the entire internal transportation.

The flow of materials and the logistics cause a considerable part of the total costs of the companies. This essentially influences the company's performance results. For the success of your business plan you should therefore ensure that the essential goals of the logistics are achieved, namely to provide:

- the exact materials,
- at the exact time,
- in the exact quantity,
- at the exact place,
- at minimum costs and
- in proper quality.

11.3 Key questions

- *What is the share of the purchasing volume compared to the turnover?*
- *How many suppliers do you work with?*
- *How has the number of the suppliers changed over the last three years? Has it decreased or increased?*
- *How far are you dependent on individual suppliers?*
- *How can you compensate the loss of a key supplier?*
- *What is the delivery reliability of your key suppliers like?*
- *Have you got perennial supply agreements?*
- *Are your purchasing conditions more favourable, identical or worse than those of the main competitors?*
- *Do you use the internet for purchasing; do you place advertisements on an electronic market?*
- *Do you regularly check new purchasing sources for raw materials, half-finished products and delivery parts?*
- *Have you got free choice in suppliers or are you strongly bound to the favours of your customers?*
- *Do you have an analysis for purchasing at you disposal?*
- *Are the qualifications of the employees in the purchasing department appropriate?*
- *How do you control that the employees of your procurement department do not become dependent on particular suppliers?*
- *How do the recording and scheduling of the customer orders into your system occur?*
- *Do you have a continuous workflow system or several independent systems?*
- *Does the indoor marketing activities have (for make-to-stock manufacturing) a prompt view over stocks and production orders as planned for the next weeks?*
- *Can customers order electronically?*

- *Does operation planning or your production planning system have access to the current stocks for precursors and finished goods?*

- *How are repeat orders of precursors processed?*

- *Are there minimum lot sizes? Who defines them?*

- *Is the finished product the responsibility of logistics or sales?*

- *Are there discrepancies between the numbers, which appear in the billing system and the manufactured quantities as feedback reported by the production?*

- *Do you have a central warehouse or several local distribution centres?*

- *Has your stock increase or decreased within the last three years?*

- *Is the transportation of goods a matter of customer responsibility (call system)? Do you engage hauliers or do you provide your own fleet?*

- *Have you handed over the entire transportation field to a haulier?*

- *Do your customers frequently complain about damages incurred during transportation or under-batches?*

- *Are error frequency and complaints lower or higher than those of your main competitors?*

- *Which dispatch and product distributing systems do your competitors use?*

- *Do you believe that you are better or worse with the overall system of your order processing, manufacturing and logistics than your main competitors?*

- *What are the essential differences in comparison with your competitors?*

12 Finance

The chapter finance is one of the most important parts within your business plan. Once you, or those responsible for the project, have worked through the different themes from the initial business idea to the different parts of the plan, it is necessary for you to consider the finances – the so called "hard facts" – on the basis of those parts.

To establish a direct link to practical financial management this chapter will, in parts, refer to a fictitious company. This will be shown with balance sheets, income statements, cash flow statements and various other planning tables. The past shall be shown in years one to three and the planning period in years four to eight.

12.1 Presentation of financial situation

Financial management, as is carried out in a business plan, is essential for every company. The process of collecting the plan's data puts the management in a position that enables it to identify weak points as well as opportunities that present themselves more quickly.

The type of finances which have to be prepared for your business plan depends to a large extent on the development stage of your company, as well as, the goals you want to achieve with your business plan. The longer a company has existed, the greater the expectations in this area are. If a company wishes to attain financing, the type and amount of the financing should generally be explained.

In the business plan components you have already described what you want to achieve on your market. You have presented your organization and management team. The company's legal framework has been defined. Your "business idea" is instilled in your product portfolio from which you want to develop and offer marketable products and services. You defined a market and customers for these products and services and developed a sales and marketing strategy. In addition to this you have shown how you manufacture and calculate your products and services.

All these activities now have to flow into an economic number system which can be used to convince your current and potential investors of your entrepreneurial ability.

In order to do this it is very important to understand the financial data system and draw up planning aids in the form of spreadsheets very early on. Though the planning of finances is no witchcraft, it does require intensive analysis on your part. In this chapter we will pay close attention to this aspect and give you such planning aids to assist you.

12.2 Financial data system

Before you begin with assumptions and plans, you need to understand the structure behind financial data systems. For many "young entrepreneurs" these systems are a necessary evil that they do not understand at all. With a financial data system, however, you will be able to show an investor that your business plan promises success. You must therefore familiarise yourself with the instruments applying to business management. Here you should by all means consult professionals to build up an effective and efficient financial data system. This will save you valuable time, which you can then devote to the enjoyment of developing and running your business.

To create a balance sheet, an income statement and a cash-flow statement you will need some basic data about your business activities. This is represented in figure 12.1.

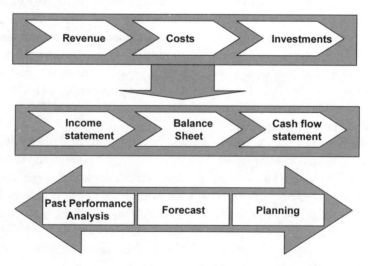

Fig. 12.1. The basic data required for financial planning.

The basic data can be classified into three categories:

- revenue,
- investments and
- costs.

The revenue is the evaluated amount of the products and services that you sell. This data is taken from your sales and marketing plan.

The investments represent the capital required for production. This can include property, buildings, machinery as well as financial investments like shares, but also immaterial investments such as computer software.

The costs include all the remaining expenses which are necessary to keep your company running: salaries, wages, office supplies, information processing, telecommunication, etc.

On the basis of this information you can create the balance sheet, income statement and cash-flow statement.

The balance sheet sums up the financial activities of your business at a key date – often coinciding with the end of the calendar year (Dec 31) – and provides you and the investors with an insight into your overall financial position. While the assets show the application of funds (the assets you have utilized for your company), the liability shows the source of funds (equity and external funds).

The income statement (sometimes referred to as the profit and loss statement, the P&L) presents the results of your business activities. The sales revenues of your products and services and all the related costs over the business year are reflected in this income statement, thus directly showing the investor your company's profitability.

The cash flow statement is especially important to the investors. It gives an idea about the company's self financing potential, i.e. which means the company has at its disposal to pay dividends, taxes, loans and interest.

Important links between the different parts of the business plan and the balance sheet, income statement and cash flow statement as well as their dependency on one another are shown in figure 12.2.

First the categories of revenue, investments and costs are elaborated and planned. These data are the basis for both balance sheet and income statement. Only with them the cash flow statement can be drawn up. We will deal with these connections more closely in the course of this chapter.

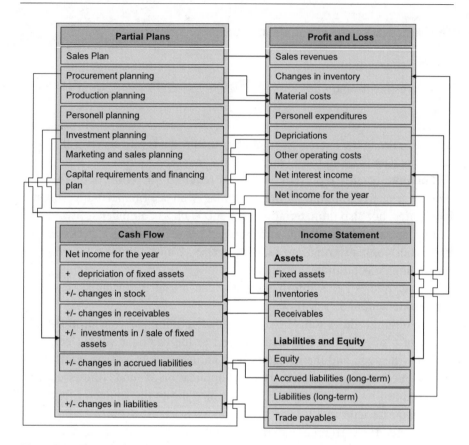

Fig. 12.2. The relationships between the plan components and the balance sheet, income statement and cash flow statement.

These statements can be calculated without great difficulty with the aid of electronic spreadsheets. Do not forget that these calculations can be used both for the past performance and for planning future activities of your company.

12.3 Analysis of economic development

Investors want to understand the current net asset position and the profitability of your company in order to gain confidence in you and your entrepreneurial abilities. Usually investors want to see the full set of financial statements of the last 3 years. Even more important for them are the planning documents the including balance sheets and income statements, as the investors can then better evaluate whether you can operate with the given capital and whether you can acquire an adequate income in the future that will result in lucrative returns for them.

Before dealing with the planning aspects you must first analyse the existing financial situation of the company because its past development must reflect a solid basis for the future. Planning should not contradict future activities but should rather be based on past activities.

You should analyse your economic situation thoroughly because this will provide you with company-specific information. Thus you recognize the strengths and weaknesses which will enable you to discover potential for improvement and take appropriate measures.

Looking back you often become aware of what you possibly did wrong. That is why it is important to be quite honest about your situation because, as you know, one learns most from one's mistakes.

Table 12.1. The balance sheet.

Assets			
	History		
	Year 1	Year 2	Year 3
A Long-term Assets	**4.806**	**4.758**	**4.571**
I. Intangible assets and prepayments	1.403	1.509	1.433
II. Fixed assets	2.799	2.694	2.739
III. Financial assets	604	555	399
B Current Assets	**20.532**	**22.149**	**24.945**
I. Inventory	13.104	14.085	13.033
II. Receivables	6.685	6.396	8.051
III. Cash	743	1.668	3.861
Total Assets	**25.338**	**26.907**	**29.516**

Liabilites and Equity			
	History		
	Year 1	Year 2	Year 3
A Equity	**4.263**	**4.940**	**4.372**
I. Share capital	1.050	1.050	1.050
II. Retained earnings	1.385	2.135	2.135
III. Current profit or loss	1.828	1.755	1.187
B Provisions	**1.447**	**1.645**	**1.899**
C Liabilities	**19.628**	**20.322**	**23.245**
I. Liabilities to banks (loans payable)	10.938	10.179	9.755
II. Accounts payable	6.602	7.152	7.501
III. Other liabilities	2.088	2.991	5.989
Total Liabilities and Equity	**25.338**	**26.907**	**29.516**

Table 12.2. The P&L.

		History		
		Year 1	Year 2	Year 3
1.	**Sales**	39.578	47.894	48.215
+/- 2.	Change in inventory	20	1.025	538
+ 3.	Other miscellaneous income	1.379	1.549	1.245
4.	**Total income**	**40.977**	**50.468**	**49.998**
− 5.	Material costs	21.868	26.541	26.750
− 6.	Personel costs	3.373	4.227	4.784
− 7.	Depreciation	657	806	901
− 8.	Other operating expenses	11.699	14.313	15.046
=	**Operating income (EBIT)**	**3.380**	**4.581**	**2.517**
+ 9.	Interest and similar income	22	12	11
− 10.	Interest and similar expenses	513	586	610
=	**Net financial income or expense**	**-491**	**-574**	**-599**
= 11.	**Income before taxes**	**2.889**	**4.007**	**1.918**
− 12.	Income taxes	1.011	1.402	671
− 13.	Other taxes	50	100	60
= 14.	**Net income / loss for the year**	**1.828**	**2.505**	**1.187**
- 15.	Increase of retained earnings	0	750	0
16.	**Net profit / loss**	**1.828**	**1.755**	**1.187**

You therefore start with an analysis of the company's financial development over the past three years. The most important tools for the analysis are the balance sheet and income statement.

In order to establish a better understanding we have provided you with a fictitious example of a balance sheet and an income statement with which we would like to give you a few analytical ideas. (Tab. 12.1 and 12.2)

As you can see from the income statement (Tab 12.2), the revenue in our example clearly rose in year 2 and then remained relatively constant in year 3. A possible reason for this development could have been, for example, the introduction of a new product in year 2 on account of which no further growth could be achieved in year 3. Looking at the net income, it strikes you that in year 3 it has declined.

A further look at the income statement shows that expenses have increased considerably in years 2 and 3, especially salaries and other expenses. It could be that the introduction of a new product accounted for an increase of employees and additional expenses.

However, you should also describe the sales trends and explain the reasons behind the development of these trends. Reasons for deviations are numerous and should be clearly analysed and explained to a third party.

Obviously, the same applies to the costs, too. It is here that you constantly have to take a close look at the development of the costs. From this you can gather:

- whether you have employed your investments wisely,

- whether you have managed your company expenditures well and

- which areas you can improve in the future.

It is mainly in your own interest to analyse the economic situation. You do not have to provide all the analyses in the business plan either, but you will have to decide clearly which information is significant for convincing the investors.

It is important that you provide the investor not only with the annual account but also with explanatory information on past developments. This information should include detailed explanations and reasons for the development of the net assets, the financing resources and the profitability.

For this purpose a key performance analysis is useful. However, you should concentrate on just a few practical key figures.

In practice, there are at least twenty to thirty well-known key figures from which you should select no more than ten meaningful figures. Appendix 1 at the back of this book contains a choice of some key figures. Make sure in your choice of figures that the investors are especially interested in the financial strength of your company. In this respect the most important figures to take into consideration include, the equity ratio, financial strength ratio, return on total assets, net debt to cash flow ratio etc.

The equity ratio shows the percentage of equity in relation to total assets. In general, the higher the equity ratio is, the more financially stable and independent a company is.

In our example (fig. 12.3) the equity ratio decreased from 18,4% in year 2 to 14,8% in year 3. The reason for this decrease is a combination of the drop in profit, which is revealed in the equity, and the simultaneous

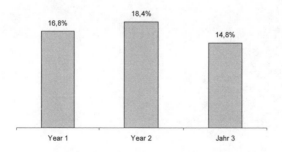

Fig. 12.3. The development of the Equity ratio using the ABC Company's balance sheets in table 12.1.

increase of the net assets. The equity (capital resources) in this example can be considered average. In order to improve this ratio in the future, you could consider not distributing the profit from the retained earnings.

The cash flow statement shows the financial strength. This statement gives information as to what extent the company has generated liquid assets. In this way the scope you have with internal financing can be estimated. In our example (Tab. 12.3) the operating cash flows from business activities increased in year 3. That means that the company has more internal capital with which to finance the business as opposed to accessing outside financing. One can also see that the investment activities have decreased significantly in years 2 and 3.

Table 12.3. The cash flow statement.

	Year 4	Year 5	Year 6	Year 7	Year 8
Net income from the Income Statement	1.118	1.601	1.061	1.910	2.902
+/- Depreciation	800	1.000	900	823	1.170
+/- Changes in provisions	8	9	2	3	3
+/- Changes in other non cash items					
Cash flow nach DVFA/SG	**1.926**	**2.610**	**1.963**	**2.736**	**4.075**
-/+ Changes in inventory	-51	-1.388	603	700	574
-/+ Changes in receivables and other assets	848	-726	-369	789	211
+/- Changes in liabilities	-2.319	343	590	1.196	1.367
Cash flows from operating activites	**404**	**840**	**2.788**	**5.421**	**6.227**
- Purchase of assets	-2.000	-650	0	-1.111	-1.900
+ Proceeds from the disposal of assets	241	370	-260	0	0
Cash flows from investing activities	**-1.759**	**-280**	**-260**	**-1.111**	**-1.900**
- Capital gains distribution	-1.187	-1.118	-1.601	-1.061	-1.910
+/- Change in long-term debt	0	-93	-56	-84	-75
Cash flows from financing activites	**-1.187**	**-1.211**	**-1.657**	**-1.145**	**-1.985**
Total cash flows	**-2.542**	**-651**	**870**	**3.165**	**2.342**

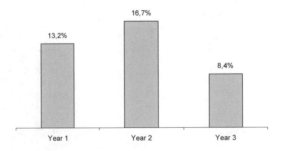

Fig. 12.4. The development of the return on total capital ratio using the balance sheets and income statements of the ABC Company (Tab. 12.2).

The return on total capital shows the productive efficiency of the company by relating the net income plus interest expense for the outside capital to the total capital (equity + liabilities). Hence it indicates the interest rate on the total capital.

In our example (fig. 12.4) the return on total capital ratio decreases. As long as the return remains above market interest rate levels, it makes sense to raise outside capital since the interest rate will be lower than the company's internal "cost of capital".

The net debt to cash flow shows how many years a company will need to be able to completely repay its net liabilities from the cash flows of the company.

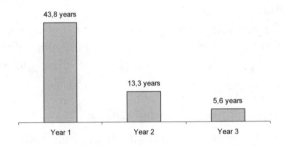

Fig. 12.5. The development of the net debt to cash flow.

The average net debt to cash flow in our example (fig. 12.5) is 5.6 years in year 3. The decrease in time in our example is due to the increase of liquid resources (cash and cash equivalents).

From the analyses of the various key figures, an evaluation can be made to assess the overall current financial position of the company. This result will give you a rough outline of the company's current financial situation. The key figures you choose to use should also represent the measures you will use to monitor, protect and improve the profits and capital of the company.

Table 12.4. Evaluation of the initial position.

Ratio	Measurement (Note)				
	Very good	Good	OK	Not good	Near insolvency
	(1)	(2)	(3)	(4)	(5)
Equity ratio	> 30%	> 20%	> 10%	< 10%	Negative
Net dept to cash	< 3 Year	< 5 Year	< 12 Year	< 30 Year	> 30 Year
Return to total	> 15%	> 12%	> 8%	< 8%	Negative

The evaluation of the initial position (Tab. 12.4) can provide only a first indication of your situation. If you have a high equity ratio as well as a high return on total assets ratio, and you can present this scenario for the future, one can assume that you will be well-positioned to deal with the opportunities and challenges that may arise in the future. With this presentation, investors will be put at ease and will place their trust in you. If your situation is not as good, you must formulate and implement appropriate measures to present a future situation of positive developments. Companies with limited capital should also be open to considering an equity investor or similar arrangements.

These analyses demand an intense and critical look at the current situation of the company and are the basis from which the company will develop in the future.

During the financial statement analysis you must also consider how the balance sheet will be presented. The use of the following different allowable accounting policies can have a significant effect on your financial statements:

- Use of options for recognition and valuation,
- Selection of straight-line or declining balance methods,
- Valuation allowances and
- Provisions.

The more qualified you are in analysing the financial development of your company, the clearer the measures will become that need to be taken. In this way you will improve the position of you company and yourself for possible credit negotiations, financing discussions or even listing your company's shares on a stock exchange.

12.3.1 Key questions

- *Are the annual accounts (balance sheets, income statements and cash flow statements) for the last 3 years available?*
- *How do you characterize your balance policies?*
- *What are your most important key figures?*
- *How have these key figures developed during the year and how do they compare to your competitors?*

- *What are the reasons for the development of these trends?*
- *Revenue*
  - *How has your revenue developed in comparison with your industry?*
  - *What are the reasons for possible deviations?*
- *Costs*
  - *What are/were the main factors affecting the development of the costs?*
  - *Is there a cost control function in your company?*
- *Net Income*
  - *How have the annual net income and the operating result (EBIT) developed in the last years?*
  - *What are the reasons for these development trends?*
- *Profitability*
  - *How have return on equity, return on total assets, and return on sales developed?*
  - *What are/were the main factors influencing the development?*
- *Liquidity*
  - *Do you regularly review the liquidity ratios (cash ratio, acid test ratio, current ratio), during the year?*
  - *How would you describe your company's payment history and that of your customers?*
- *Equity*
  - *How are you capitalized?*
  - *How does the structure of your equity compare to those of other companies?*
- *Cash flows*
  - *What are the main factors responsible for the development of the cash flows?*
  - *What were the cash flows used for in the last years?*

12.4 Company's future development

Determining the future potential of the company requires intense planning of all your entrepreneurial activities, which have been described in the preceding chapters. The estimation of the company's future earnings, as well as the strength of the balance sheet, will determine the probability that you are able to pay back creditors, as well as obtaining future credit through loans and investments. A clear and consistent development from the past into the future is a prerequisite for qualified planning.

Before you begin planning the budgets, you must collect all the data from the other parts of the business planning process. It is imperative that you have a good understanding of each of these parts. To sum up, you need the following information:

- the company strategy, which results from the strategic goals in chapter 4,
- the personnel planning, described in chapter 5,
- the product and/or product portfolio planning (chapter 6),
- the market and competition description (chapter 7),
- the sales and marketing strategy (chapter 8),
- the production plan (chapter 10), and
- the procurement and logistics plan (chapter 11).

Your financial planning is based on the information contained in these planning modules and your assumptions. Your assumptions should be realistic and comprehensible and they should have a clear and direct relation to the historical data. Take into account that a plan that presents an overly optimistic development can lead to an investor's loss of confidence if the goals presented are not reached.

A typical business plan covers five years. Plans for shorter periods of time do not provide potential investors with enough information to assess the actual potential of your company. Everything that extends over the period of five years is normally regarded as too speculative and is therefore of no additional use.

The cash flow statement, as well as the income statement, should be prepared on a monthly basis for the first two years. After that presentation on a quarterly basis would be sufficient. The balance sheet on the other hand, should be presented on a quarterly basis in the first two years and annually thereafter.

When planning, remember to comply to generally accepted accounting principles, for example IAS, US GAAP or another local GAAP[1].

A very important point is the consistency of the data within the plan. The cash flow calculation, the balance sheet and the income statement must be based on the same assumptions. For example, the estimated sales will appear in the income statement. The cash flow statement will include estimated cash flows, which must match the estimated sales, and take into consideration the terms of payment granted to the customer. In addition, receivables in the balance sheet are dependent on the sales volume, the customers' payment terms and history, as well as the volume of questionable receivables.

12.4.1 Planning the sales

Sales planning represents your appraisal of the market for the next years using past history data as your starting point. The sales data are based on the marketing planning already determined.

For the sales planning you should use the general information in chapters 6-8 covering:

- Market coverage goals,
- Pricing structures,
- Product mixing,
- Evaluation of your competitors, and
- Return assumption.

The structure of the sales planning can then be determined by at least one of the following criteria:

- Products,
- Sales areas (regions),
- Customers, as well as
- Sales force (teams).

---

[1] International accounting standards.

The sales estimates must be well-founded and plausible in order to prepare a realistic plan. Now the estimates can be prepared based upon your actual data. For this purpose we use a planning table as shown in table 12.5, abbreviated for presentation purposes.

On this occasion we have prepared a plan using a planning horizon of 5 years and will show you a section of the monthly planning for the first two years as well as the quarterly planning for years 6-8.

In our example we show two products whose sales are seasonal. Through years 4 to 8, we have adjusted the sales volumes and increased sales prices for each product. We have adjusted the sales prices according to the increase in demand during each year. The planned revenues find expression in the income and loss statement.

Determining accurate sales estimates for the future is usually one of the most important tasks, as the sales estimates are the starting point for all other activities defined in your business plan. In any case you should clearly explain the basis for your sales estimates. The sales estimates must correspond to your description of the market, the marketing strategy and your anticipated position on the market, as you have described them in the chapters market and marketing. Your market share, for example, should be consistent with your estimates of the entire market size and your competitive advantage over your competitors.

It is precisely in the early years of a company that the sales are frequently planned on the basis on sales volumes. If you choose this approach, you should present your assumptions with regard to volume growth, initial price per unit and the timing of price increases. Since many products are subject to seasonal volume fluctuations, it is important to find and present specific assumptions that demonstrate that these factors have been taken into account in the planning.

You can also plan your sales as a percentage increase in value each month. In this case you should describe the percentages and the reasons for the corresponding increases or decreases in these percentages. Companies that have been in business for a number of years usually use this percentage method to plan their sales.

If you offer different product lines or services and the composition of the product lines changes in the course of time, you should provide separate forecastings and assumptions for each product line. Depending on the type of your product you sell, you should also take into account possible product returns. If you use middlemen for sales, you must also take into account the amount of unsold products that may be returned to you.

Table 12.5. The sales estimates.

	Year 4					
	Product A			Product B		
	Number of items	Price per item	Sales	Number of items	Price per item	Sales
Month 1	1.200	0,200	240	7.500	0,420	3.150
Month 2	1.200	0,200	240	7.450	0,420	3.129
Month 3	1.200	0,200	240	7.400	0,410	3.034
Quarter 1	3.600		720	22.350		9.313
Month 4	3.500	0,400	1.400	7.100	0,390	2.769
Month 5	6.000	0,450	2.700	4.800	0,390	1.872
Month 6	6.000	0,450	2.700	3.900	0,390	1.521
Quarter 2	15.500		6.800	15.800		6.162
Month 7	12.000	0,500	6.000	3.900	0,390	1.521
Month 8	12.000	0,500	6.000	3.800	0,390	1.482
Month 9	7.000	0,350	2.450	4.800	0,390	1.872
Quarter 3	31.000		14.450	12.500		4.875
Month 10	1.200	0,200	240	5.750	0,420	2.415
Month 11	1.100	0,200	220	7.200	0,430	3.096
Month 12	1.100	0,200	220	7.900	0,430	3.397
Quarter 4	3.400		680	20.850		8.908
Total	53.500		22.650	71.500		29.258
Total	51.908					

	Year 8					
	Product A			Product B		
	Number of items	Price per item	Sales	Number of items	Price per item	Sales
Month 1						
Month 2						
Month 3						
Quarter 1	4.262	0,280	1.194	26.116	0,438	11.439
Month 4						
Month 5						
Month 6						
Quarter 2	17.702	0,455	14.620	18.576	0,410	7.612
Month 7						
Month 8						
Month 9						
Quarter 3	30.924	0,473	14.620	14.096	0,410	5.779
Month 10						
Month 11						
Month 12						
Quarter 4	3.825	0,368	1.407	23.057	0,448	10.334
Total	56.713		25.280	81.845		35.155
Total	60.435					

12.4.1.1 Key questions

- *Are your assumptions consistent, in particular with your market analysis and the information from the other chapters of your business plan?*
- *Have you kept to your marketing and sales goals from the respective planning modules?*
- *How will your sales volumes develop in 3 to 5 years?*
- *How do you plan your volumes and/or sales?*
    - *Through your sales force*
    - *Through your sales manager*
    - *Through your management*
- *According to which criteria do you plan your sales volumes and/or sales?*
    - *By products*
    - *By sales areas (regions)*
    - *By customer or customer type*
    - *By sales force*
- *Have you developed planning worksheets for the respective criteria you have used to plan your sales volumes and/or sales?*
- *How have you considered the external influences that can affect your plans?*
    - *External influences (inflation rate, political and tax changes etc.)*
    - *Competition influences (prices, market position etc.)*
    - *Internal influences (sales capacity, product design, pricing policy etc.)*
- *Do you plan revenue reductions?*
    - *Discounts, Boni, Skonti*
    - *Commissions*
    - *Other sales' costs (royalties, shipping costs, transportation costs etc.)*

12.4.2 Cost planning

Instead of planning the costs as a percentage of the sales, you should rather determine the material, personnel and other operating costs. Your cost planning should be based on the marketing and production plans that you have already developed and should include all the detailed cost elements.

Determine the details of the costs per product on the basis of the estimates of the production department. The production department should supply the details of the material requirements along with the costs from supplier price quotes. These costs normally include raw materials and supplies as well as purchased products and services. You should plan these costs on a monthly basis.

You should also keep in mind industry specific factors when you are planning the material costs (Tab. 12.6). For a trading company the number of items and prices are the main factors while a production company must additionally anticipate all the costs needed to produce the finished product. Take into account seasonal demands on your products which can impact your material planning. If you have several product lines, it makes sense to plan the unit costs per product line separately. Explain the factors which influence the price per unit. A production expansion, for example, can lead to lower purchase prices since larger amounts can be bought and thus quantity discounts can be negotiated. Market changes and seasonal factors can substantially influence the costs. You should consider these circumstances in the sales planning as well and therefore carry out the cost planning on a monthly basis.

Table 12.6. The planning of the material costs.

	Year 4							
	Month 1			...	Month 12			Total
	Number of items	Price per Item	Expense	...	Number of items	Price per Item	Expense	
Product A				...				
Raw materials and supplies	1.200	0,130	156	...	1.100	0,130	143	1.794
Purchased goods	1.200	0,111	133	...	1.100	0,111	122	1.532
Total Product A			289	...			265	3.326
Product B				...				
Raw materials and supplies	7.500	0,100	750	...	7.900	0,110	869	9.714
Purchased goods	7.500	0,167	1.253	...	7.900	0,168	1.327	15.483
Total Product B			2.003	...			2.196	25.197
Total			2.292	...			2.461	28.523

We have provided a simply formulated material cost plan in our example. We made an assumption in the example that prices would remain unchanged during the entire year. We plan to adjust the prices in the following years with the average rate of inflation. At the end of the planning, we take the total cost amount of T€ 28.523 to the appropriate position in the income statement.

In planning the personnel costs, the costs are based upon the number of employees you now employ and/or intend to employ (Tab. 12.7). You should plan your employee costs (wage, salary and social costs etc.) by functional areas and first determine the requirements for the next months or years. You can use average costs when you are not certain of wage and salary amounts for future employees but again you are encouraged to be as detailed as possible in order to provide a good basis for future analyses. During further annual planning, you should also take into account increases in wages and salaries, bonuses as well as possible changes of payroll fringe costs.

In our example we show the first and last months in the 12 month planning table. We have planned the costs by functional areas and have shown the gross salary employer-paid social costs. Following the marketing and

Table 12.7. The planning of personnel costs.

	Month 1			...	Month 12			
	No. of Employees	Gross salary per Employee*	Personnel cost	...	No of Employees	Gross salary per Employee*	Personnel cost	Total
Management	2	13,0	26	...	2	14,3	29	328
Purchasing	13		47	...	16		61	650
Supervisor	1	7,0	7	...	1	7,4	7	86
Dept head	2	5,0	10	...	4	5,1	20	182
Clerks	10	3,0	30	...	11	3,1	34	382
Production	21		71	...	22		73	862
Supervisor	1	6,0	6	...	1	6,4	6	74
Technical	4	5,0	20	...	3	5,1	15	212
Clerks	16	2,5	40	...	18	2,6	46	515
Administration	2	2,5	5	...	2	2,6	5	61
Sales support	38		172	...	48		231	2.419
Supervisor	2	8,0	16	...	2	8,6	17	199
Field sales	20	5,5	110	...	25	5,9	147	1.543
Sales support	6	3,5	21	...	10	3,7	37	351
Call-Center clerks	10	2,5	25		11	2,7	29	327
R & D	5		31	...	6		39	417
Supervisor	1	10,0	10	...	1	11,0	11	126
Technical	3	6,0	18	...	4	6,1	24	255
Assistant	1	3,0	3	...	1	3,1	3	36
Accounting	2		11	...	2		12	135
Supervisor	1	7,5	8	...	1	8,0	8	93
Accountant	1	3,5	4	...	1	3,6	4	43
Controlling	3		15	...	3		16	190
Supervisor	1	9,0	9	...	1	9,7	10	112
Controller	2	3,2	6	...	2	3,3	7	78
Total	84		373	...	99		460	5.001

* incl. Employer paid social insurances

sales planning, we intend to strengthen the sales department and tend to employ additional employees in the future. We have planned the development of the other functional areas conservatively in order to keep the personnel costs low. The resulting costs are also reflected in the income and loss statement.

To manufacture and market your products you need machines and production resources that are subject to use and therefore being depreciated according to the life of the machines. These fixed assets are recorded in a fixed asset schedule showing the deduction for each machine based upon the useful life of the machine. These depreciation costs are reflected in the income and loss statement and reduce the value of the fixed assets correspondingly in the balance sheet.

Those materials required for productivity are known as investments. Investments are very important for each company because they are usually expensive and long-term. Therefore you must consider very carefully what investments you wish to make. (Tab. 12.8).

There are different types of investments, namely:

- Material investments,

- Financial investments,

- Immaterial investments,

Table 12.8. The planning of the investments.

| | Life of asset (yr) | Year 4 | | | | ... | Year 8 |
		Month 1	Month 2	...	Total	...	Total
Investments							
Franchise licenses, patents, software			200	...	200	...	
Property				...	0	...	
Buildings				...	100	...	
Machinery and equipment		1.000		...	1.700	...	1.500
Sales and office equipment				...	0	...	400
Total		1.000	200	...	2.000	...	1.900
Depreciation and Amortisation							
Franchise licenses, patents, software	4	0	4	...	46	...	68
Property		0	0	...	0	...	
Buildings	30	0	0	...	2	...	3
Machinery and equipment	7	12	12	...	163	...	161
Sales and office equipment	4	0	0	...	0	...	100
Total		12	16	...	125	...	332

- Replacement investments,
- Expansion investments and
- Modernizing investments.

With each investment you must be aware of whether and in what period of time your investment will pay itself off. Therefore you should ask yourself some important questions with each investment you make:

- How high is the investment?
- How can you finance the investment (out of cash flows, cash resources, borrowed funds)?
- What is the expected yield (return on the asset)?
- How long is the payback period?
- What risks are you taking (technical and financial risks)?
- What are the tax effects?

You should describe the largest objects of investment (assets) that you wish to acquire and when you plan to acquire them. You must then estimate the expected economic lifetime of those assets and estimate the sum of the monthly/annual depreciation. If you intend to lease equipment, remember to plan these expenses within the other operating expenses.

Table 12.9. The liquidity plan.

	Year 4			
	Month 1	Month 2	...	Month 12
Receipts				
Sales revenue	3.390	3.369	...	3.617
Other income	106	150	...	112
Interest income	1	1	...	1
Total receipts	3.497	3.520	...	3.730
Disbursements				
Material costs	2.292	2.278	...	2.461
Personnel costs	373	378	...	460
Other operating costs	1.518	1.331	...	1.238
Interest expense	73	82	...	83
Investment costs	1.000	200	...	0
Debt repayments	100	100	...	100
Total disbursemnts	5.356	4.369	...	4.342
Liquidity cover	-1.859	-849	...	-612

For the first budget year we assume a monthly investment of T€ 2,000. For the technical assets and machines we assume a service life of 7 years and for the software, a service life of 4 years, which means a monthly depreciation of T€ 12. This investment leads to a financing requirement of T€ 1,000 in month 1 of year 4 (year 4 being the first year of our budget). We must then take a look at our liquidity plan to see what the monthly financing options are.

The liquidity plan basically is a revenue and expense statement, which means that payment flows are shown (Tab. 12.9). The cash receipts side shows your settled accounts and miscellaneous receipts. At this point you should consider carefully the payment behaviour of your customers because a time span exists between the time in which you send the bills and the time when you receive the payments. On the expenditure side all your payments are shown including payments to suppliers for products and services, wages and salaries, interest expense, investment costs, etc.

Back to our example, in illustration 12.9 you can see a liquidity deficit of T€ 1,859 that we must finance. We decide to finance the investment by

Table 12.10. The interest and debt repayment plan.

	Year 4			...	Year 8
	Month 1	Month 2	...	Total	Total
Debt repayment plan					
Credit facilities					
Available line of credit	15.000	15.000	... 15.000	...	18.000
Beginning balance	7.498	8.357	... 7.498	...	9.678
+ Additional credit taken	859	624	... 2.214	...	721
- Pay backs			... 1.347	...	
= Ending balance	8.357	8.981	... 8.365	...	10.398
Loans					
Beginning balance	2.257	3.157	... 2.257	...	2.024
+ Addtional loans	1.000	200	... 1.200	...	1.099
- Repayments	100	100	... 1.200	...	925
= Ending balance	3.157	3.257	... 2.257	...	1.949
Interest					
Credit facilities					
Average amount outstanding	7.928	8.669	... 7.931	...	10.038
Interest rate	9,00%	9,00%	... 8,11%	...	7,82%
Interest expense	59	65	... 643	...	784
Loans					
Average amount outstanding	2.707	3.207	... 2.257	...	1.987
Interest rate	6,00%	6,00%	... 5,69%	...	5,62%
Interest expense	14	16	... 127	...	112
Interest expense	73	81	... 771	...	896

raising an external credit (long-term loan) of T€ 1,000. We will finance the difference of T€ 859 by claiming our advance on current account loan.

By having raised a loan we must work out an interest and debt repayment plan (Tab. 12.10).

We calculate the interest cost by taking the average outstanding loan balance (opening balance – ending balance / 2) multiplied by the interest rate (using the monthly rate) that we expect to get. We calculate and record the interest cost in the income statement.

After determining the interest payable, we now turn to the other company operating costs (Tab. 12.11). These include, for example, rent, office supplies, communication costs, advertising costs, travel related costs, insurance, as well as legal, consulting and auditing costs.

Table 12.11. Planning of other operating costs.

	Year 4					Year 8
	Month 1	Month 2	...	Total	...	Total
Rent	165	165	...	1.980	...	2.148
Leasing	250	250	...	2.904	...	3.194
Utilities (heating, etc.)	33	33	...	396	...	444
Office materials	30	30	...	360	...	382
Telephone, Fax, Internet, Postage	15	15	...	180	...	239
Auto costs	11	11	...	132	...	149
Shipping and transportation costs	300	300	...	3.600	...	3.672
Advertising	300	300	...	3.750	...	4.500
Travel	34	47	...	700	...	764
Repair and maintenance	70	70	...	817	...	841
Insurance	150		...	300	...	336
Legal and consulting	100	50	...	315	...	515
Financial statements and audit costs	0		...	45	...	49
Other costs	60	60	...	720	...	756
Total	**1.518**	**1.331**	...	**16.199**	...	**17.989**

The company's other operating costs require somewhat more time to be prepared because you must consider all the other costs that can occur during the entire course of the year. You can see in table 12.11 that we have planned considerable expenditure for buildings and leasing as well as advertising and shipping costs. If, for example, you require large warehouses, possibly at different locations, you may need to rent these, as is the case in our example. We have also decided on leasing the majority of the machines and equipment facilities. Our product requires considerable advertising activities as well as shipping and transportation costs. We have also planned these exactly in other operating costs. When we have finished gathering the data and estimating the costs, we add the annual amount to the corresponding sections of the income statement.

You should be aware that it is precisely in the phase of entering the market, that the marketing and sales costs are very important and can also be extremely high because you must introduce your new products to the customers and the market in general in such a way that you create an interest in and a demand for your product. For the first two years you should work out a detailed plan based on your work in chapters 7 and 8. This plan should contain the necessary personnel and marketing costs (sales commissions, exhibition costs and costs for promotional campaigns, etc.). For the following years the marketing costs can be estimated as a percentage of the sales.

Investors see research and development (R&D) costs as an investment in the future. In planning R&D costs you have great discretionary powers. Take into consideration that these costs present a decisive indicator for the long-term and sound growth of your business. If your product has a high margin and a short life span, investing in important R&D is crucial for the continual development of new products. Therefore the budgeting should be based on a detailed plan. This plan should contain the products to be developed in future, required personnel and all the other necessary costs.

If R&D costs for the development of a product play only a minor role, you can assume that the R&D costs will represent a percentage of the sales. Remember that R&D costs can also be of great importance to many service companies.

A further planning component is the realistic planning of taxes. First estimate the tax rate for each year. Think of all the different types of taxes that apply to your company in your jurisdiction (income tax, trade tax, corporation tax, etc.). Then apply this rate to the monthly profit before tax.

If you have losses in the first years, you can use the accumulated deficit in order to pay less or no taxes in the following year(s).

Due to the complexity of tax laws, you are recommended to seek the advice of a tax consultant who will assist you with your tax calculations.

12.4.2.1 Key questions

- *Have you coordinated your sales and production plans?*

- *What delivery obligations do you have in regard to your customers?*

- *Would it be better to purchase certain in order to avoid possible bottlenecks in production?*

- *What stock-levels of raw materials and supplies do you need for a smooth production?*
- *What price trends do you expect especially for your most important raw material?*
- *What type of warehouse and production capacities do you need?*
- *How can you react to certain sales peaks?*
- *How will you guarantee the financing of the inventory?*
- *What do you plan to do in order to expand the production capacity?*
- *What requirements will be made on your production regarding:*
  - *Labour force*
  - *Machines*
  - *Logistics*
- *Would it cost less to outsource some activities?*
- *How many employees do you need?*
  - *Managers*
  - *Skilled staff*
  - *Unskilled employees*
- *What wages and salaries arise?*
- *How do wages and salaries develop?*
  - *Wage agreements*
  - *Wage increases*
  - *Overtime arrangements/regulations*
  - *Vacation arrangements, holidays,*
  - *Insurance, social costs*

12.4.3 Planning the balance sheets and the P&L

Now that you have planned your costs you are in a position to convince your investor of your future entrepreneurial activities. The investor will receive a detailed picture about your sales, investments and your company operating costs concerning the time elapsed. So now we turn to planning the balance sheets and income statements in order to present the overall future position of your company.

Table 12.12. The planning of the assets.

		Plan				
		Year 4	Year 5	Year 6	Year 7	Year 8
A	**Long-term Assets**	**5.510**	**5.155**	**4.515**	**4.803**	**5.533**
I.	Intangible assets and prepayments	1.532	1.427	1.267	1.224	774
II.	Fixed assets	3.819	3.569	3.089	3.420	4.600
III.	Financial assets	159	159	159	159	159
B	**Current Assets**	**21.606**	**23.069**	**23.704**	**25.380**	**26.937**
I.	Inventory	13.084	14.472	13.869	13.169	12.595
II.	Receivables	7.203	7.928	8.296	7.507	7.296
III.	Cash	1.319	669	1.538	4.704	7.045
Total Assets		**27.116**	**28.224**	**28.219**	**30.183**	**32.470**

As already mentioned, you will need the balance sheets over a period of several years. From this perspective the investor can see how your assets and liabilities have developed and what financing requirements you will have in future.

Let us begin with the asset side of the balance sheet which in turn is divided into the fixed assets and the current assets (Tab. 12.12).

The fixed assets are subdivided into immaterial, material and financial assets. With the help of a mirror of assets (Table 12.13) find out the intakes and dispatches of the assets and then transfer the net booking values into the balance sheet. All of the fixed assets are based on your planning of your investments and are shown in the balance sheet at their net book values (net of depreciation).

We have already calculated the investments and the depreciation in Table 12.8. These items are now the components of the fixed asset schedule.

The new investments flow into the column avenues of acquisition and production costs. The acquisition and production costs at the beginning of the year and the avenues as well as the disposals amount in the gross book value. The difference between gross book values and cumulative depreciations result in net book values, which are transferred into the appropriate position of the fixed asset.

The funds tied down in current assets should not be underestimated. The current assets are composed of inventory, receivables, stocks and liquid funds.

Estimate the inventory required to be prepared for you planned turnovers. The inventory planning depends on the length of the manufacturing process and can be expressed as the turnover ratio (e.g. the inventory is turned over four times a year) or production cycle (for example three

Table 12.13. The fixed asset schedule.

	Gross book value				Accumlated depreciation				Net book Value
	Beginning Year 1	Additions	Reductions	Ending Year 1	Beginning Year 1	Additions	Reductions	Ending Year 1	Ending Year 1
I. Intangible assets and repayment									
1. Franchise licenses	240,00	60,30	20,40	279,90	168,00	33,80	3,80	198,00	81,90
2. Goodwill	77,30	1.320,00	0,00	1.397,30	38,50	36,50	0,00	75,00	1.322,30
3. Prepayments	10,00	0,00	10,00	0,00	0,00	0,00	0,00	0,00	0,00
	327,30	1.380,30	30,40	1.677,20	206,50	70,30	3,80	273,00	1.404,20
II. Fixed assets									
1. Land and buildings	2.648,50	188,20	18,00	2.818,70	691,60	187,30	15,90	863,00	1.955,70
2. Mach. and equip.	0,00	0,00	0,00	0,00	0,00	0,00	0,00	0,00	0,00
3. BGA	1.839,10	478,90	191,30	2.126,70	1.067,80	399,70	182,70	1.284,80	841,90
4. Assets under construction	1,20	1,00	1,30	0,90	0,00	0,00	0,00	0,00	0,90
	4.488,80	668,10	210,60	4.946,30	1.759,40	587,00	198,60	2.147,80	2.798,50
III. Financial assets									
1. Shares in affiliated companies	135,80	0,00	0,00	135,80	120,80			120,80	15,00
2. Loans to affiliated companies	0,00	0,00	0,00	0,00	0,00			0,00	0,00
3. Investments in equities	413,50	0,00	101,50	312,00	0,00			0,00	312,00
4. Loans to associate companies	0,00	0,00	0,00	0,00	0,00			0,00	0,00
5. Investments in equities	0,00	0,00	0,00	0,00	0,00			0,00	0,00
6. Other loans	323,80	0,00	42,30	281,50	4,00			4,00	277,50
	873,10	0,00	143,80	729,30	124,80	0,00	0,00	124,80	604,50
Total	5.689,20	2.048,40	384,80	7.352,80	2.090,70	657,30	202,40	2.545,60	4.807,20

months). The timing of the purchase of required raw materials plays an important role in planning the liquidity demands.

With regard to the receivables, estimate the time period between the origin of the turnover (invoice generated) and the payment of the invoice (cash received). This can be referred to as "average period of receivables" (e.g. 60 days) or as "turnover ratio of receivables" – e.g. a turnover ratio of six corresponds to an average period of receivables of 60 days. Industry statistics can serve as good guidelines for the average period of receivables.

The cash and bank balances show the liquid assets that you have and from which you can pay your short-term financial obligations. Most entrepreneurs prefer to keep enough cash on hand in order to enable them to operate independently for at least *3* months in case unexpected problems arise.

The liability side of the balance shows how your assets are financed. To put it in a nutshell, this side consists of your equity plus outside capital (Tab. 12.14). As you know, the more outside capital you need, the more significant the equity becomes. If, for example, you plan to invest considerably within the next years, you must arrange the liability side accordingly.

In the stage of establishing your business you should try and raise as many own resources as possible because, in early stage businesses, investors are cautious and you will be lucky to receive even small amounts of financing from outside investors. It is only when your business model proves reliable (proves itself on the market) and shows prospect for future

Table 12.14. The planning of the liability side of the balance.

Liabilites and Equity					
		Plan			
	Year 4	Year 5	Year 6	Year 7	Year 8
A Equity	**4.303**	**4.786**	**4.246**	**5.095**	**6.087**
I. Share capital	1.050	1.050	1.050	1.050	1.050
II. Retained earnings	2.135	2.135	2.135	2.135	2.135
III. Current profit or loss	1.118	1.601	1.061	1.910	2.902
B Provisions	**1.914**	**2.024**	**2.105**	**2.189**	**2.277**
C Liabilities	**20.900**	**21.414**	**21.868**	**22.899**	**24.107**
I. Liabilities to banks (loans payable)	10.622	10.859	11.090	11.702	12.348
II. Accounts payable	8.076	8.256	8.436	8.906	9.402
III. Other liabilities	2.202	2.299	2.342	2.291	2.357
Total Liabilities and Equity	**27.117**	**28.224**	**28.219**	**30.183**	**32.470**

growth, that you will be able to convince investors of providing your business with credits.

In your planning you should look closely at all financing options that you have. Many start-up companies have failed due to inadequate financing. In particular poor liquidity is one of the main reasons of insolvency.

The equity section represents the owners' invested capital in the company either from the company itself (reinvested profits), or from the partners and stockholders who were convinced of and believed in your business idea and hope for above average returns on their investments. You should consider early in your planning process whether it is necessary to obtain investment capital to develop your business.

Regarding companies that have already been active and profitable for several years the question of how to distribute the profits arises. Although it is attractive to take profits from the company, one should consider creating profit reserves in order to improve one's own surplus. Particularly service companies with only small property holdings at their disposal should show a considerable equity position.

If you issue common or preference shares, you should describe the sources of supply for your required capital. If you have issued shares, state the number of shares and the issue prices of the shares. If in future you plan to source financing through investment financing or venture capital, state the required capital as well as the estimated date when the funding will be needed. The number of shares and the share prices will then depend on the future development of your company.

In our example we have assumed that the profit is distributed annually. Since no additional equity is being added in the next years, the equity will remain constant apart from the annual fluctuations of the net income.

Let us have a look at the liabilities. Here the liabilities are classified as short-term and long-term. This applies to loans and provisions as well as normal operating payments.

First, estimate the period of time in which you pay your bills. A start-up company should try to pay its bills punctually in order to earn a good reputation. Therefore, in planning, you should consider using a payment period that is a little shorter than the industry average. In planning the liabilities, the term of credit is expressed in days. If salary payments represent one of your main costs, consider including the monthly payments in your liquidity planning.

Referring to our example and to the interest and repayment plan (Table 12.10) our short-run liabilities increase due to the availment of the credit line. The increased final amount is reflected in the corresponding position of the balance sheet.

Long-term liabilities are bank loans, loans, mortgages, etc. which have a term of more than a year. In these positions you plan the outside capital which you need from each investor.

Since we will finance our investments with a loan, the final amount of the loans rises according to our interest and repayment plan, which flows to the corresponding line items relating to loans from banks.

Table 12.15. The planning of the income statement.

	Plan				
	Year 4	Year 5	Year 6	Year 7	Year 8
1. **Sales**	51.908	53.070	54.221	57.244	60.435
+/- 2. Change in inventory	-75	786	-93	-732	-574
+ 3. Other miscellaneous income	1.277	1.309	1.342	1.375	1.410
4. **Total income**	**53.110**	**55.165**	**55.470**	**57.887**	**61.271**
− 5. Material costs	28.523	29.162	29.814	30.482	31.164
− 6. Personel costs	5.001	5.113	5.317	5.424	5.532
− 7. Depreciation	800	1.000	900	823	1.170
− 8. Other operating expenses	16.199	16.561	16.892	17.315	17.989
= **Operating income (EBIT)**	**2.587**	**3.329**	**2.547**	**3.843**	**5.417**
+ 9. Interest and similar income	12	12	12	48	78
− 10. Interest and similar expenses	771	788	805	849	896
= **Net financial income or expense**	**-759**	**-776**	**-793**	**-801**	**-818**
= 11. **Income before taxes**	**1.828**	**2.553**	**1.754**	**3.042**	**4.598**
− 12. Income taxes	640	894	614	1.065	1.609
− 13. Other taxes	70	58	79	67	87
= 14. **Net income / loss for the year**	**1.118**	**1.601**	**1.061**	**1.910**	**2.902**
- 15. Increase of retained earnings	0	0	0	0	0
16. **Net profit / loss**	**1.118**	**1.601**	**1.061**	**1.910**	**2.902**

After having completed the balance sheet, you can now attend to planning the Income statement. Now the total amounts of sales and expenses are taken from the detailed planning to the corresponding positions in the Income statement (Table 12.15). From those figures the gross profit is calculated. If you then subtract the financial outcome, which is the result of the interest and repayment plan, you will get the normal business operations. You then hate to apply the effective income tax rate of your country from that result.

12.4.3.1 Key questions

- *How have the assets, liabilities, equity, finance and profit situation developed starting from the last balance sheet date up to the setting of your business plan?*

- *Is the presentation of the development of the assets, liabilities, equity, and finance and profit situation consistent with the interim financial situation since the last balance sheet date?*

- *Will the planned equity capital and the long-term external capital be sufficient to finance the fixed assets?*

- *Did you plan the inventory depending on the sales estimates?*

- *What range of materials do you need for the manufacturing of your products?*

- *How high are your inventories?*

- *According to which criteria do you plan the inventory?*
  - *Procurement time*
  - *Inventory turnover*
  - *Turnover ratio*
  - *Turnover of raw materials and supplies*
  - *Inventory as a percentage of current assets*
  - *Inventory as a percentage of the balance sheet total*

- *According to which criteria do you plan the receivables?*
  - *Receivables turnover*
  - *Range of receivables*

- *What will the capitalization of your company look like in the future?*

- *Which factors affect the equity structure of your company?*

- *Do you need further equity?*
- *Does an increase in capital come into consideration?*
- *How will the equity capital change due to your financing requirements?*
- *Do you plan to retain or distribute your future profits?*
- *Is there an investment accumulation at your company?*
- *Which investments do you wish to finance externally and which internally?*
- *How do you assess the future payment behaviour of your suppliers?*
- *Which provisions must you provide for?*
  - *Provisions for pensions/retirement*
  - *Vacation*
  - *Royalties*
  - *Guarantee claims*
  - *deferred taxes*
- *Which factors have the greatest influence on the development of the annual net income and operating result?*
- *Which factors will have the greatest influence on equity, total capital and sales profitability?*
- *Have you calculated several scenarios in order to consider the influence of different developments on your plan? (See also chapter 12.5 sensitivity and risk analysis.)*

12.4.4 Planning the cash flow

The next step is to show the development of the future cash flow. The financial and assets position is not sufficient to convince the providers of capital or potential investors. The investor will want to get a general idea about your financial strength.

The cash flow calculation (Table 12.16) is acquired from the planned income and loss statement, the budgeted balance sheet, the investment planning, the profit appropriation and the terms of interest and redemption. This calculation does not require any new assumptions and can be derived from the existing plans.

Table 12.16. The planning of the cash flow.

	Year 4	Year 5	Year 6	Year 7	Year 8
Net income from the Income Statement	1.118	1.601	1.061	1.910	2.902
+/- Depreciation	800	1.000	900	823	1.170
+/- Changes in provisions	8	9	2	3	3
+/- Changes in other non cash items					
Cashflow nach DVFA/SG	**1.926**	**2.610**	**1.963**	**2.736**	**4.075**
-/+ Changes in inventory	-51	-1.388	603	700	574
-/+ Changes in receivables and other assets	848	-726	-369	789	211
+/- Changes in liabilities	-2.319	343	590	1.196	1.367
Cash flows from operating activites	**404**	**840**	**2.788**	**5.421**	**6.227**
- Purchase of assets	-2.000	-650	0	-1.111	-1.900
+ Proceeds from the disposal of assets	241	370	-260	0	0
Cash flows from investing activities	**-1.759**	**-280**	**-260**	**-1.111**	**-1.900**
- Capital gains distribution	-1.187	-1.118	-1.601	-1.061	-1.910
+/- Change in long-term debt	0	-93	-56	-84	-75
Cash flows from financing activites	**-1.187**	**-1.211**	**-1.657**	**-1.145**	**-1.985**
Total cash flows	**-2.542**	**-651**	**870**	**3.165**	**2.342**

You should consider the following factors which can positively influence your cash flow:

- the reduction of receivables,
- the sale of inventory and fixed assets,
- the later payment of liabilities and
- the raising of credit (short- and long-term).

Of course, if you do the opposite of the above-listed points your liquidity decreases accordingly.

In our example, especially due to the investments made and reduction of the short-term liabilities, we show a negative cash flow in year 4. We have designed our plans so that the cash flow rises slowly and thus our internal financing is strengthened.

12.4.4.1 Key questions

- *How will the cash flow develop within the next years?*
- *What shall the cash flows be used for in future?*
- *How many years will be required to pay back all the debts from the cash flows?*

Now you have completed the entire financial model and you have before you all the actual data and all the plan data. The plan data in particular should be subjected to a critical examination. For this the sensitivity analysis that we present in the next section would be suitable.

12.5 Sensitivity and risk analysis

The reliability of your planning depends on how well considered your assumptions are and which risks your company is prone to. Investors attach particular importance to a presentation that considers different scenarios or incidents and shows how you will deal with potential risks. In writing this section of your business plan, you should analyse the critical assumptions of your planning as well as the possible risks.

By means of the sensitivity and risk analysis you can consider what actions you would take if there were deviations from your assumptions in the plan, or if you found yourself exposed to risks that were not included in the plan.

The sales assumptions are to be considered as a critical figure in most companies. If you estimated a sales increase of 50 %, what would be the result of a sales increase of "only" 30%? Or what if the costs were 5% higher than assumed? For start-up companies concrete milestones are very important. What will happen if a product cannot be launched at the planned time, 3 months later, for instance?

Fig. 12.6. The different risk groups.

According to the probability of their arising and the estimated extent of damage different risks can be established using a matrix. The art of risk analysis consists of remaining objective, being conscious of potential threats and being able to try to understand fictitious scenarios.

The risk matrix will help you to identify the risk areas, characterize the risks, and then respond appropriately to them. With this analysis you show your investors that not only do you clearly recognize the risks, but also have the ability to respond to them.

In general the risk profile consists of eight different risk groups (Fig. 12.6).

In the business plan presentation you do not have to include complete financial planning (with balance sheets, income statements and cash flow statements) for every eventuality. It is sufficient to subject the most critical assumptions to a general analysis and discuss the alternative results in a continuous text. An important point to focus on is whether additional financing is required and how the profitability and return on equity will have developed at the end of your planning timeframe.

The first financial plan you develop will take a lot of time to complete. This time is only well-spent if you are able to provide the reader of your financial plan with sufficient and qualified information so that he can judge the future perspectives of your company realistically.

12.5.1 Key questions

Market risks

- How do you judge a threat to the company due to:
- product substitution?
- demographic changes?
- new trends?
- sudden loss of purchasing power in the relevant markets?
- sudden loss of a relevant market?
- surprising means taken by your competitors?
- to what extent is the product portfolio endangered by technical and scientific innovations?

Personnel risks

- How do you judge a threat to the company due to:
- employees?

- the working atmosphere?
- inadequate employee qualifications?
- lack of confidentiality and loyalty of employees?
- organizational shortcomings?
- high employee turnover?
- resigning of key personnel?
- accidents at work?
- high rate of absences due to illness?
- business interruptions?
- work stoppages?
- obsolescence of the management or the staff?
- threatening indemnities by third parties?

Economic risks

- How do you judge threats to the company due to:
- incorrect production quantities and too high inventories?
- fluctuating purchase prices which you can not pass on to your sale prices?
- inadequate quality, customer complaints and necessary replacement services?
- transportation risks?
- weaknesses in your distribution channels or due to your competitors' use of new distribution channels?
- sudden breakdown in the sale prices?
- loss of receivables?
- delivery agreements or completion dates, which you cannot meet?

Technical risks

- How do you judge a threat to the company due to:
- vandalism?
- necessary value adjustments?
- unforeseen work stoppages and interruptions in production?

- incorrect production planning?
- material related production disturbances?
- employee related production interruptions?

Financial risks

- How do you judge a threat to the company due to:
- economic cycles?
- liquidity bottlenecks?
- developments on the financial markets?
- developments on the money markets?
- imprecise financial planning?
- uncertain financing measures?
- costs for unforeseen guarantees?
- necessary, but unforeseen research and development costs?
- necessary, but unforeseen investments?
- necessary guarantee payments?

Administrative risks

- How do you judge a threat to the company due to:
- deficient production preparation?
- production errors?
- insufficient production controls?
- inadequate controlling instruments?
- administration errors?
- inadequate intern controls?
- problematic strategy decisions?
- management errors?
- location disadvantages (costs, employee qualifications, infrastructure)?
- deficiencies in or destructions to the EDP system?

Commercial risks

- How do you judge a threat to the company due to:

- political measures?
- social groupings or individuals?

Environmental risks

- How do you judge a threat to the company due to:
- environmental risks such as weather influences or epidemics?

Preventative measures

- How do you judge the competence of your preventative measures?
- How do you judge the height of equity loss in the worst case scenario?
- How do you judge the probability of the worst case?

12.6 How finance experts rate planning

Usually potential investors first examine whether the planning and the assumptions made are plausible. Experienced investors are usually very quick in doing so. If the figures appear reasonable, they carry out further test analyses. In the next section we would like to present some of these analyses to you.

12.6.1 Margins

Investors calculate your operating margins (gross profit and operating profit) and calculate research and development, marketing and administration costs as a percentage of the sales. They compare your results with the values of other companies in your industry. If, for instance, you estimate a gross profit of 65 % whereas other companies achieve only 50 %, investors will question your assumptions and reasoning. You should be prepared to defend your figures.

12.6.2 Asset management

This is an area that many managers ignore. Your budgeted balance sheets should show that you understand how to manage liquid assets, receivables and inventory. This is very important for potential investors and bankers.

In general your planning and key figures should be comparable to those of other companies in your industry. Various industry consultants and studies are available for comparative purposes.

12.6.3 Company valuation

Investors usually estimate the value of a company on the basis of the planned profits at the end of a certain period (usually 3 to 5 years). The profit at the end of this period is then multiplied by a factor specific to the industry. For this there are no generally valid rules. If, for instance, you are operating in a growth industry, this factor often lies between 10 and 20. In an established enterprise investors could use a factor of between 5 and 10. These factors help to estimate the future value of your company. The investor then discounts this future value with a deduction for risk in order to estimate the current value of your company.

For example, a company with an annual turnover of 40 Mio. € has a profit of 6 Mio. € at the end of 5 years. The investor multiplies the 6 Mio. € with the factor 10, resulting in a company valuation of 60 Mio. €. This would be the value for the company if, for example, one was looking to raise funds on the stock exchange or to sell the company to a third party. There are two reasons why this number interests investors in particular:

- The company is to be big enough one day to make the investment worth, and

- Investors use this number in order to determine how big the investor's share must be in order to justify the financing desired by you.

12.7 Financing request

Companies that are looking for financial support must take care in formulating their request in the finance section. You should indicate how much money you will need, why you need it and what you are going to do with it. Here are a few general points that you should consider:

State how, in accordance with your financial planning, you intend to use the financing. If you state that the money is to be used as start-up capital to finance new products and services and to establish a distribution organization, these costs should be clearly documented in your financial plan. If you require a second or third round of financing, you should be able to refer to the detailed explanations in your financial plan. Nevertheless, the thing to do would be to give a short explanation of how much money will be used for research and development, marketing, production, capitalization and so forth.

You require leeway during the later phase of the plan. When you consider how much money you will need, calculate a little leeway as flexibility, so that your enterprise does not find itself in trouble in case deviations occur.

Interactions with the capital structure must be taken into account. If your company is already operating, you should explain the capital structure and what effect the suggested financing will have on that structure. If you are a start-up company, state how you got the start-up capital, who the investors and/or part-owners are, what their positions are in the company, what percentage of the shares these people own and how much they paid for their interests.

Describe additional financing schemes. You should also explain further plans of how you meet your financing requirements, except venture capital, private capital or loan financing. Many companies obtain a credit line or a loan from a bank, or finance their fixed assets through leasing arrangements. Your tax consultant or lawyer will usually have many contacts with banks or other institutions where you can apply for short-term financing.

The equity rate must be right. In order to decide how much you will finance with a credit and how much you will finance through equity you must weigh up many points. Financing capital with a credit can be less expensive. To do that, however, you must be in a position to pay back this money and to provide sufficient securities. The more is financed by a credit, the less attractive you will become for potential investors or financiers. Therefore, pay attention that credit financing does not outweigh equity financing. The more credit financing you have, the less flexible you will become and your ability to obtain more money in future will be limited. Your tax consultant can help you to find a good combination of credit and equity financing.

Describe your requirements for future financing concisely and clearly. If the development of your project requires several years, you might only receive financing gradually. When will you need follow-up financing and what are the milestones that you have to reach by then? Do you wish to use credit financing? If so: when, how much and on which terms?

12.7.1 Key questions

- Are your assumptions consistent with the other sections of your business plan?

- Which basic financing principles (for example the principle of self-financing, external financing, internal financing or outside financing) is your company pursuing over the next years and with what measures will these basic principles be realized?

- How much capital will you need, from which date and for how long?

- What type of financing are you looking for?

- How quickly can your company obtain credit when required?

- How will you use the received funds?

- How many percent of the profit were retained in the last years?

- What percentage of the profit do you plan to distribute in the next 5 years?

12.8 Repayment and exit-strategy

Investors will want to know the rate of return they can expect for their investment. Different investors also have different expectations. Rates of return that are acceptable for banks will not convince a venture capital financier. Financiers also consider different investment periods: in general venture capital financiers will want to sell your investment in a manageable period of time. This is also called "exit" of an investor. The thing to do is to actively suggest an exit-strategy to the investor. Banks, on the other hand, plan longer redemption periods for their guaranteed loans.

13 The way to the investor

If in 12 chapters we have succeeded in describing why and how you develop your business plan, a thirteenth chapter would merely raise the question of how you would actually take the potential investor on board, bearing in mind all that you have at hand.

Where and how do you begin the struggle for the right investor? How
do you conduct and manage the smooth process of these negotiations? Finally, how do you master your success? The search for and the choice of
financing alternatives, as well as the task of convincing banks and investors, presents a daily challenge to us. There are three reasons for this:

- Your daily business cannot be put in hold.
- The capital market shows no mercy.
- The future is always uncertain.

The key to success lies solely in careful preparation. Two thirds of all financing processes fail even before the first bank is contacted.

Raising capital is often too great a challenge for managers to meet in
addition to all the strain of everyday business life, the whole process being
extraordinarily difficult to manage. Nonetheless, in order to achieve the
best solution in this difficult situation, it is essential to adapt a pro-active,
disciplined and methodical approach:

- Plan your financial strategy.
- Prepare yourself carefully for the funding process.
- Involve the investor.

13.1 Planning the financial strategy

To stay in control of the funding process, you need a sound finance strategy
for negotiations in advance. You simply need to know what you want and
actually expect from the funding process. It is precisely this awareness of

the process that enables you to aim for the best financing option and to prepare and position the company for the involvement of the investors. Take a step back to consider the end of the game:

- Clarify your company's position.
- What is my position?
- Work out a realistic strategic plan:
- What am I aiming at?
- How much capital do I require?
- When do I require the capital?
- Identify your financing options:
- What sources of capital are available?

13.1.1 What is your company's position?

Before planning a financial strategy, you need to go through a sound gathering of information and a process of rationalization that will give you a complete picture of your company's current position. This effort should produce a coherent picture of the company that is consistent its future development.

Furthermore, this process will also help to identify strategic obstacles which your company cannot overcome by itself and for which you will need support. These obstacles can be financial, operational or market-related.

13.1.2 A realistic business plan

Once all the requisite information has been collected and validated, you should then, as already described in chapters 4 to 12, develop a business plan that shows in detail what goal your company intends to reach and how you plan to do so. The business plan should:

- Begin by clearly formulating the goals and direction of your company,
- describe each area of the company with regard to its contribution to costs and revenues, and
- provide a standardized picture of the company's finances including a statement for the last three and next five years' development.

The business plan is not just a means of raising funds, but rather helps you to consider your company from a strategic point of view. In addition to this, it offers you a schedule for the company's future.

For this reason it should not be a document that is merely adorned with glorious references and pictures a promising yet deceptive future. It should rather be a realistic appraisal and assessment of your company, and should show that you are aware of the weaknesses and strengths, i.e. the risks and opportunities of your proposed venture.

13.1.3 Identifying the financing options

With a strategic plan at hand, that establishes

- where you are positioned,
- what you aim at,
- what you require

in order to achieve your goals, you can start considering which financing alternatives best suit your business idea.

The company's growth stage presents the first criterion for deciding which type of financing is possible.

A company passes through different development stages:

- Seed,
- Start-up and
- Growth.

In each of these stages there is a choice of different financing alternatives. In order to be able to envisage the appropriate financing source for your company, various factors have to be considered. Here three aspects come to the fore.

The first aspect refers to shareholding:

- Are the existing owners or shareholders prepared to give up some of their influence and to what extent?
- Is your company able to amortize the debts?
- Has your balance sheet the required strength to bear fluctuations in interest, repayments and liabilities?

The second aspect refers to the value chain:

- What is the search for talented employees based on in your company?

- Does your company have to obtain special access to potential customers, suppliers and strategic partners?

- Are you looking for an investor who can also act as a strategic partner?

Finally, the third aspect refers to a successful long-term relationship with investors:

- What level of commitment and involvement do you expect of your investor?

- Are you looking for investors who will continue their financial support in the future?

13.2 Preparing for the funding process

With the strategic plan at hand and a general investment direction chosen, you will be able to begin preparing your company for the funding process.

How? You should put your company through the same rigorous review it will face from future investors. The managing directors should analyse the company from the perspective of potential investors with regard to its profitability and the "Return on Investment" (ROI). This is called *due diligence process*.

The following test can be of help to you.

13.2.1 Presenting the organizational structure

The most important criterion for an investor with regard to carrying out the business plan successfully is, as shown in chapter 5, the "quality of the management team"

- Does the management have the necessary experience which is essential for successful leadership?

- Can the company attract and retain qualified employees?

13.2.2 Assessment of the business model

You should be in the position to show the investor that your company is focused on a profitable, attractive and growing market. If you want a 100% guarantee that you will get funded, develop a convincing list of reference customers. (see chapter 4).

This does not only refer to customers who have already purchased. Should your product still be in development, focus on your potential customers.

- Is your company aiming at a profitable, specific, attractive and growing market?
- Does your company actually have customers?
- Do the existing stakeholders actively support the company?

13.2.3 Validation of the financial package

As already stated in chapter 8, be prepared to support historical and projected cash-flow statements, P&L statements and balance sheets with a level of detail beyond that included in the annual statement.

Work out a sales model that thoroughly breaks down revenue by products, services, regions and sales staff. Draw up a corresponding model of the costs, too.

When preparing financials, you should take into consideration the time frame within which your potential investors wish to liquidate their holdings. Showing that the possibility of an exit at a foreseeable point of time has been taken into account within the calculations, will have a significant impact on private equity investors, for whom the timing of exit presents a major risk factor.

- Is the potential ROI worth your time, effort and resources?
- Are revenue and cost assumptions supported with sufficient details?
- Is the possibility of the investor's exit ensured in foreseeable time?

13.3 Involve the investor

Negotiating with investors is like being on a roller coaster:

- the intensity of the first interview,

- the elation at their confirmation

- the deep satisfaction after concluding the deal.

In spite of the strongly fluctuating emotions in both you and your investors, you should adhere systematically to continuity in order to get your company successfully over this hurdle.

The time and special effort dedicated to pro-active planning and preparation will involve the investors in a process that your company can then control.

Along the process of involving the investor you aim consistently and focused at four rules:

- First: Be choosy! Do not agree to everything.

- Second: Go shopping for your deal! Approach it with the same perceptiveness as when you go shopping.

- Third: Negotiate the details!

- Fourth: Close, collect and reflect!

13.3.1 Shopping a deal

To create a competitive combination of possible investors for a successful transaction, it is essential to approach at least five investors on average.

Bear in mind, however, that members of the investment community talk to each other. So you should beware of making controversial statements.

Always compare supply and demand. Be consistent when pursuing the goal of establishing an intense relationship with the investor most suitable in your case.

Investors who wish to have a share do not only focus on the management team but also on the development, performance and strength of your finances. However, there is no historical data available for venture investors, since the relevant companies are still in an early stage of development.

13.3.2 Negotiating details

Even if negotiations begin with the first interview, intensive negotiations do not begin until the third or fourth meeting.

Your goal is to extract a term sheet from at least two of the possible investors. Focus, in a disciplined manner, on the structure of the deal and on how the financing can influence the carrying out of your company's strategic plan.

Consider future financing possibilities and their impact on the investor, among these the preference ranking of financing options as well as the shifting of shareholding on account of further future investors' entries.

13.3.3 "Close, collect and reflect"

With the end in sight, do not become complacent or overconfident. Keep pushing until the money is on your bank account. Negotiations can unexpectedly and radically change up to the last minute due to changes of the market or the company's value and thus investors change their minds.

When the meeting has finished, the documents are signed and the paying off has been effected, you should take the opportunity of thinking about the whole procedure once more. Examine the entire process critically and evaluate it carefully with regard to your business idea. In retrospect, work out where your strengths and weaknesses lie, and what could have been done more effectively.

Throughout the process, you should constantly maintain an excellent relationship with the investors, even those who rejected your plan and those whom you rejected, for the future will always remain uncertain.

Key performance indicators

Investors determine a number of key figures for the evaluation of the net assets, financial position and results of operations in the past as well as for budgeting. The following key figures support you in analysing the net assets:

The equity ratio indicates the share of equity within the total capital. The higher the ratio, the more creditworthy a company is. On account of this the structure of equity plays a crucial role within the credit-rating of banks.

$$\text{Equity ratio} = \frac{\text{Total equity x 100}}{\text{Total assets}} \qquad \text{(Eq. A.1)}$$

The debt ratio indicates the amount of debt (liabilities to banks, trade and other liabilities) as a proportion of the whole company's financing. The higher this ratio, the less willing the banks are to give additional loans.

$$\text{Dept ratio} = \frac{\text{Short - term, mid - term, long - term debt x 100}}{\text{Total assets}} \qquad \text{(Eq. A.2)}$$

The total asset turnover indicates how many times capital invested in the total assets has been turned over. This figure provides an indicator of how productively capital has been utilised within the company. The more often capital has been turned over, the more efficient the assets have been utilised for the generation of sales.

$$\text{Total asset turnover} = \frac{\text{Sales}}{\text{Total assets}} \qquad \text{(Eq. A.3)}$$

The receivables turnover indicates how many days on average lie between the generation of sales and the payment of receivables. The feasibility of your assumptions regarding the planned payment terms can be derived from this figure. It can also be an indication of how well your accounts receivable management works.

$$\text{Receivable turnover} = \frac{\text{Total trade receivables x 360}}{\text{Sales}} \qquad \text{(Eq. A.4)}$$

The equity to assets ratio is also referred to as "the golden balance sheet rule". Long-term assets have to be financed by long-term available capital. The proportion of coverage should not be less than 100% over a longer period.

$$\text{Equity to assets ratio} = \frac{\text{Total equity} + \text{long - term borrowings}}{\text{Assets}} \text{ x } 100 \quad \text{(Eq. A.5)}$$

The investment ratio indicates the volume of new investments in tangible fixed assets in the expired period proportional to acquisition and production costs as at the beginning of the period. Thus it becomes clear, indirectly, what percentage of the fixed assets has not been reinvested. If this figure decreases over several years, this could imply that the fixed assets are obsolete. The higher this figure, the newer the machines held by a company and the more secure its future is.

$$\text{Investment ratio} = \frac{\text{Net investments in tangible fixed assets x 100}}{\text{Tangible fixed assets at the start of the period}} \qquad \text{(Eq. A.6)}$$

The fixed asset intensity indicates fixed assets as a proportion of total assets. This ratio can only be used as a reliable indicator where compared with others in the sector. Production companies naturally have, for example, more fixed assets than service providers. On comparing industries, if an enterprise has a lower fixed asset intensity this could indicate that fixed assets are obsolete. If fixed assets intensity is too high compared to others this could be negative since, fixed assets are usually difficult to sell where there are shortages of liquidity.

$$\text{Fixed asset intensity} = \frac{\text{Fixed assets x 100}}{\text{Total assets}} \qquad \text{(Eq. A.7)}$$

The current asset intensity shows current assets as a proportion of total assets. As for fixed asset intensity a clear assessment can only be made on the basis of a comparison with other enterprises in the same sector. A high proportion of current assets can indicate high liquidity since these can usually be sold quickly. However, a very high level of this ratio can indicate, for example, that inventories are too high.

$$\text{Total revenue per employee ratio} = \frac{\text{Sales}}{\text{Average number of employees}} \quad \text{(Eq. A.8)}$$

The following key figures support you in the analysis of your financial position:

The retained earnings to average equity indicates the proportion of the retained earnings to average equity available.

$$\text{Retained earnings to average equity} = \frac{\text{Retained earnings x 100}}{\text{Average equity}} \quad \text{(Eq. A.9)}$$

whereby average equity is defined as:

$$\text{Average equity} = \frac{\text{Equity period 1} + \text{Equity period 2}}{2} \quad \text{(Eq. A.10)}$$

This ratio can, for example, give a potential investor an indication of where investments will be made.

The liquidity ratio I indicates which percentage of the short-term liabilities can be repaid via liquid assets (cash balances, bank balances, cheques and bills of exchange). This figure usually is lower than 100%. The significance of this ratio is relatively restricted.

$$\text{Liquidity ratio I} = \frac{\text{Cash and cash equivalents x 100}}{\text{Short term liabilities}} \quad \text{(Eq. A.11)}$$

The liquidity ratio II should, if possible, not be lower than 100%, so that the company will not have financial difficulties.

$$\text{Liquidity ratio II} = \frac{\text{Total current assets - inventories}}{\text{Short term liabilities}} \times 100 \quad \text{(Eq. A.12)}$$

The liquidity ratio III should at the latest exceed the value of 100%. If this is not the case, an equivalent financing period cannot be guaranteed for total assets and this could lead to payment difficulties. Certain fixed assets might possibly be used to pay liabilities. If these fixed assets cannot be sold quickly enough this could lead to insolvency or, if fixed assets are sold, to a great deal of disruption in production.

$$\text{Liquidity ratio III} = \frac{\text{Total current assets x 100}}{\text{Short term liabilities}} \quad \text{(Eq. A.13)}$$

The net debt to cash flow indicates how many years a company needs to amortize their debts under the premise of a constant cash flow. An increasing time of amortizing debts can lead to a decrease of an investors' willingness to offer additional capital. The effective level of indebtedness is calculated by subtracting liquid assets, stocks within current assets and short-term liabilities from the outside capital.

$$\text{Net debt repayment rate} = \frac{\text{Net debt}}{\text{Cash flow}} \qquad \text{(Eq. A.14)}$$

The following key figures support you in analysing your results of operations:

The return on sales indicates how high the share of profit is according to your sales revenue. This figure indicates how effective the cost management of an enterprise is. The higher this figure, the better an enterprise is prepared for externally driven cost increases or income reductions such as, e.g., increasing purchase prices due to scarcity of raw materials or price wars on the income side.

$$\text{Return on sales} = \frac{\text{Net income x 100}}{\text{Sales}} \qquad \text{(Eq. A.15)}$$

The return on equity indicates the return on total equity in the past period. This figure is very important for an investor who wants to take a holding in your company. It shows him the return on the invested capital. For an investor this figure has to be higher than the market interest level plus a risk premium, otherwise a holding in the company is of no interest to him.

$$\text{Return on equity} = \frac{\text{Net income x 100}}{\text{Average total equity}} \qquad \text{(Eq. A.15)}$$

The return on total assets gives information about how effectively fixed and other assets are used to generate surpluses. Furthermore it indicates if it is worth using borrowings to finance assets. If the interest rate for the borrowings is lower than the return on total assets, the use of borrowings has proved worthwhile.

$$\text{Return on total assets} = \frac{\text{Net income + interest expenses}}{\text{Total assets}} \text{ x } 100 \qquad \text{(Eq. A.16)}$$

The return on investment determines the efficiency of the capital employed. The return on sales is multiplied by the total asset turnover (see ratios above). In this ratio the efficiency of the cost management is compared in relation to the productivity of the capital employed.

$$\text{Return on investment} = \frac{\text{Net income x 100}}{\text{Sales}} \times \frac{\text{Sales}}{\text{Total assets}} \quad \text{(Eq. A.17)}$$

The cost of material to sales indicates the proportion of the cost of materials to the total sales of the company. In addition to rises in raw material prices, an increasing proportion of cost of materials compared to other periods can also be caused by an increase in rejects from production.

$$\text{Cost of material to sales} = \frac{\text{Cost of materials x 100}}{\text{Sales}} \quad \text{(Eq. A.18)}$$

The personnel expense ratio indicates the share of personnel expenses within the company's total sales. In comparison to the cost of materials ratio it can be ascertained if a company is material intensive or personnel-intensive. By means of this information one can evaluate if the company is more susceptible to risks from the purchasing markets (e.g. rising raw material prices) or to personnel risks (e.g. staff turnover). Reasons for an increasing personnel expense ratio could be, for example, rising wages and salaries costs not passed on to sales prices or social security changes. However, if this ratio decreases compared from period to period, this could, e.g, be caused by an increase in productivity by the production function.

$$\text{Personell expense ratio} = \frac{\text{Personell expenditure x 100}}{\text{Sales}} \quad \text{(Eq. A.19)}$$

The total revenue ratio indicates how much sales revenue can be allotted in a period to each employee. This figure is used by providers of capital to, in comparison to other competitors, to make the budgeted number of employees reasonable in comparison to budgeted revenues.

$$\text{Total revenue per employee ratio} = \frac{\text{Sales}}{\text{Average number of employees}} \quad \text{(Eq. A.20)}$$

List of abbreviations

GAAP	General accepted accounting principles
IAS	International accounting standard
KPI	Key performance indicators
RMS	Relative market share
ROI	Return on investment
SMEs	Small and medium sized enterprises
USP	Unique selling proposition

List of figures

List of tables

Further reading

Chapter 1-3

Anatomy of a Business Plan: A Step-by-Step Guide to Building a Business and Securing Your Company's Future (Anatomy of a Business Plan) (Paperback) by Linda Pinson ; 304 pages; Kaplan Business; 6 edition (November 1, 2004); ISBN-10: 0793191920; ISBN-13: 978-0793191925.

Building A Successful Business Plan: Advice From The Experts (Socrates Answers) (Paperback) by Socrates Media (Editor); 272 pages; Socrates Media; Bk&CD-Rom edition (September 30, 2005); ISBN-10: 1595462430; ISBN-13: 978-1595462435.

Business Plans Handbook: A Compilation Of Actual Business Plans Developed By Business Throughout North America (Business Plans Handbook) (Hardcover) by Lynne Pearce (Editor); 459 pages; Thomson Gale (November 4, 2005); ISBN-10: 0787666815; ISBN-13: 978-0787666811.

The Business Plan Workbook (Sunday Times Business Enterprise Guide) (Paperback) by Colin Barrow , Paul Barrow , Robert Brown ; 398 pages; Kogan Page; 5 edition (July 1, 2005); ISBN-10: 0749443464; ISBN-13: 978-0749443467.

The Instant Business Plan 3rd Edition, Twelve Quick and Easy Steps to a Successful Business; Includes free downloadable MACINTOSH/ WINDOWS business plan software (Paperback) by Paul Kirschner ; 144 pages; Puma Publishing; 3rd edition (March 15, 2000); ISBN-10: 0940673428; ISBN-13: 978-0940673427.

The Prentice Hall Encyclopedia of Model Business Plans (Paperback) by Wilbur Cross , Alice M. Richey ; 448 pages; Prentice Hall Press; Bk&CD Rom edition (September 30, 1998); ISBN-10: 0735200246; ISBN-13: 978-0735200241.

The Rule Book of Business Plans for Startups (Psi Successful Business Library) (Paperback) by Roger C. Rule ; 336 pages; Entrepreneur Press; 1 edition (January 1, 2000); ISBN-10: 1555715192; ISBN-13: 978-1555715199.

Writing a Convincing Business Plan (Paperback) by Arthur R. De-Thomas Ph.D., Lin Grensing-Pophal; 272 pages; Barron's Educational Series; 2 edition (January 1, 2001); ISBN-10: 0764113992; ISBN-13: 978-0764113994.

Writing Business Plans That Get Results (Paperback) by Michael O'Donnell; 160 pages; McGraw-Hill; 1 edition (April 1, 1991); ISBN-10: 0809240076; ISBN-13: 978-0809240074.

Chapter 4

Corporate Financial Strategy, Second Edition (Paperback) by Ruth Bender, Keith Ward; 416 pages; Butterworth-Heinemann; 2 edition (July 15, 2002); ISBN-10: 0750648996; ISBN-13: 978-0750648998.

Corporate Level Strategy (Hardcover) by Goold, Alexander, Campbell; 464 pages; John Wiley & Sons (February 1, 2001); ISBN-10: 0471047163; ISBN-13: 978-0471047162.

Corporate Strategy: A Resource Based Approach (Paperback) by David J. Collis, Cynthia A Montgomery; 240 pages; McGraw-Hill/Irwin; 1 edition (October 1, 1997); ISBN-10: 0072895438; ISBN-13: 978-0072895438.

Corporate Strategy (Paperback) by Collis; 256 pages; OPEN UNIVERSITY PRESS (January 1, 2005); ISBN-10: 0071111077; ISBN-13: 978-0071111072.

Corporate Strategy (Paperback) by David J. Collis, Cynthia A Montgomery, David Collis, Cynthia Montgomery; 256 pages; McGraw-Hill/Irwin; 2 edition (July 17, 2004); ISBN-10: 0072312866; ISBN-13: 978-0072312867.

Financial Times Corporate Strategy Casebook (Paperback) by Philip A. Wickham; 428 pages; Financial Times Management (June 2000); ISBN-10: 0273643428; ISBN-13: 978-0273643425.

Oxford Handbook of Strategy Volume 2 by David O. Faulkner, Andrew
    Campbell; 552 pages; Oxford University Press, USA; 1st edition
    (June 15, 2002); ISBN-10: 0199248648; ISBN-13: 978-0199248643.

Strategy Safari (Paperback) by Henry Mintzberg, Bruce W. Ahlstrand,
    Joseph Lamprel, Joseph Lampel; 416 pages; Financial Times Pren-
    tice Hall (July 20, 2001); ISBN-10: 0273656368; ISBN-13: 978-
    0273656364.

The Oxford Handbook of Strategy Volume 1 by David O. Faulkner,
    Andrew Campbell; 1064 pages; Oxford University Press, USA;
    New edition (May 15, 2006); ISBN-10: 0199275211; ISBN-13:
    978-0199275212.

Translating Corporate Strategy Into Project Strategy: Realizing Corpo-
    rate Strategy Throught Project Management (Paperback) by Peter
    Morris, Ashley Jamieson; 116 pages; Project Management Institute
    (December 30, 2004); ISBN-10: 1930699379; ISBN-13: 978-
    1930699373.

Translating Strategy into Action (Leading from the Center) (Hardcover)
    by Duke Corporate Education; 112 pages; Kaplan Business (August
    1, 2005); ISBN-10: 0793195209; ISBN-13: 978-0793195206.

Chapter 5

A Handbook of Human Resource Management Practice 10th Edition (Pa-
    perback) by Michael Armstrong; 982 pages; Kogan Page; 10 edition
    (May 1, 2006); ISBN-10: 0749446315; ISBN-13: 978-0749446314.

Business Process Management: Practical Guidelines to Successful Im-
    plementations (Hardcover) by John Jeston, Johan Nelis; 464 pages;
    Butterworth-Heinemann (April 24, 2006); ISBN-10: 0750669217;
    ISBN-13: 978-0750669214.

Business Process Management Systems: Strategy and Implementation
    (Hardcover) by James F. Chang; 304 pages; AUERBACH (Septem-
    ber 9, 2005); ISBN-10: 084932310X; ISBN-13: 978-0849323102.

Designing Dynamic Organizations: A Hands-On Guide for Leaders at All
    Levels (Paperback) by Jay Galbraith, Diane Downey, Amy Kates;
    286 pages; AMACOM/American Management Association (No-
    vember 2001); ISBN-10: 0814471196; ISBN-13: 978-0814471197.

Designing Organizations: An Executive Guide to Strategy, Structure, and Process Revised (Hardcover) by Jay R. Galbraith; 192 pages; Jossey-Bass; 2nd edition (November 15, 2001); ISBN-10: 0787957453; ISBN-13: 978-0787957452.

Harvard Business Review on Leadership (Harvard Business Review Paperback Series) (Paperback) by Henry Mintzberg, John P. Kotter, Abraham Zaleznik, Joseph Badaracco, Charles Farkas, Ronald Heifetz, Donald Laurie; 238 pages; Harvard Business School Press (September 1998); ISBN-10: 0875848834; ISBN-13: 978-0875848839.

Harvard Business Review on Managing People (Harvard Business Review Paperback Series) (Paperback) by Rob Goffee, Garetht Jones, Sterling Livingston, Jeffrey Pfeffe, David Thomas, Robin J. Ely,, Jean-Frantois Manzoni, Jean-Louis Barsoux, 269 pages; Harvard Business School Press (February 1999); ISBN-10: 0875849075; ISBN-13: 978-0875849072.

Harvard Business Review on What Makes a Leader (Paperback) by Daniel Goleman, Michael MacCoby, Thomas Davenport, John C. Beck, Dan Clampa, Michael Watkins; 210 pages; Harvard Business School Press; 1ST edition (October 15, 2001); ISBN-10: 1578516374; ISBN-13: 978-1578516377.

HR Answer Book, The: An Indispensable Guide for Managers and Human Resources Professionals (Hardcover) by Shawn A. Smith, Rebecca A. Mazin; 256 pages; AMACOM/American Management Association; 1st edition (March 2004); ISBN-10: 0814472230, ISBN-13: 978-0814472231.

Essential Business Process Modeling (Paperback) by Michael Havey; 332 pages; O'Reilly Media (August 18, 2005); ISBN-10: 0596008430; ISBN-13: 978-0596008437.

Human Resource Management: Gaining A Competitive Advantage (Hardcover) by Raymond A. Noe; 736 pages; McGraw-Hill Companies; 5th edition (January 2005); ISBN-10: 0072987383; ISBN-13: 978-0072987386.

Human Resources Business Process Outsourcing: Transforming How HR Gets Its Work Done (Jossey Bass Business and Management Series) (Hardcover) by Edward E. Lawler, Dave Ulrich, Jac Fitz-enz, James

Madden, Regina Maruca; 272 pages; Jossey-Bass (August 12, 2004); ISBN-10: 0787971634; ISBN-13: 978-0787971632.

Leadership and Self Deception: Getting Out of the Box (Paperback) by Arbinger Institute, The Arbinger Institute (Author); 192 pages; Berrett-Koehler Publishers; Reprint edition (February 9, 2002); ISBN-10: 1576751740; ISBN-13: 978-1576751749.

Leadership in Organizations (Cram101 Textbook Outlines – Textbook NOT Included) (Paperback) by Yukl; 196 pages; Academic Internet Publishers; 5th edition (October 19, 2006); ISBN-10: 1428810390; ISBN-13: 978-1428810396.

Managing Human Resources (Cram101 Textbook Outlines – Textbook NOT Included) (Paperback) by Bohlander, Snell; 356 pages; Academic Internet Publishers, Inc. (October 18, 2006); ISBN-10: 1428810102; ISBN-13: 978-1428810105.

Process Management (Hardcover) by Jörg Becker, Martin Kugeler Michael Rosemann; 370 pages; Springer; 1 edition (August 13, 2003); ISBN-10: 3540434992; ISBN-13: 978-3540434993.

Structure in Fives: Designing Effective Organizations (Paperback) by Henry Mintzberg; 312 pages; Prentice Hall; 1 edition (June 30, 1992); ISBN-10: 013855479X; ISBN-13: 978-0138554798.

Trust Me: Developing a Leadership Style People Will Follow (Hardcover); 256 pages; WaterBrook Press; 1st edition (January 20, 2004); ISBN-10: 1578567548; ISBN-13: 978-1578567546.

The 21 Indispensable Qualities of a Leader: Becoming the Person Others Will Want to Follow (Hardcover) by John C. Maxwell; 160 pages; Nelson Business (June 1, 1999); ISBN-10: 0785274405; ISBN-13: 978-0785274407.

The Structuring of Organizations (Hardcover) by Henry Mintzberg; 512 pages; Prentice Hall; 1 edition (December 28, 1978); ISBN-10: 0138552703; ISBN-13: 978-0138552701.

Women and the Leadership Q: Revealing the Four Paths to Influence and Power (Hardcover) by Shoya Zichy; 310 pages; McGraw-Hill; 1 edition (August 29, 2000); ISBN-10: 0071352163; ISBN-13: 978-0071352161.

Chapter 6-8

Basic Marketing w/Student CD (Hardcover) by Jr., William D. Perreault E. Jerome McCarthy, Joseph P. Cannon; 790 pages; McGraw-Hill/Irwin; 16 edition (October 12, 2006); ISBN-10: 0073324043; ISBN-13: 978-0073324043.

Business Intelligence Using Smart Techniques: Environmental Scanning Using Text Mining and Competitor Analysis Using Scenarios and Manual Simulation (Paperback) by Charles Halliman; 224 pages; Information Uncover (January 1, 2006); ISBN-10: 0967490634; ISBN-13: 978-0967490632.

Cases to Accompany Contemporary Strategy Analysis (Paperback) by Robert Grant; 392 pages; Blackwell Publishing Limited; 5 edition (January 1, 2005); ISBN-10: 1405124083; ISBN-13: 978-1405124089.

Competitive Advantage: Creating and Sustaining Superior Performance (Hardcover) by Michael E. Porter; 592 pages; Free Press; 1st Free P edition (June 1, 1998); ISBN-10: 0684841460; ISBN-13: 978-0684841465..

Competitive Strategy: Techniques for Analyzing Industries and Competitors (Hardcover) by Michael E. Porter; 397 pages; Free Press; 1 edition (June 1, 1998); ISBN-10: 0684841487; ISBN-13: 978-0684841489.

Contemporary Strategy Analysis: Concepts, Techniques, Applications (5th Edition) (Paperback); by Robert M. Grant; 560 pages; Blackwell Publishing Limited; 5 edition (January 1, 2005); ISBN-10: 1405119993; ISBN-13: 978-1405119993;

Customer Loyalty: How to Earn It, How to Keep It (Paperback) by Jill Griffin; 272 pages; Jossey-Bass; Rev Sub edition (October 9, 2002); ISBN-10: 0787963887; ISBN-13: 978-0787963880.

Customer Relationship Management (Hardcover) by Federico Rajola; 160 pages; Springer; 1 edition (May 7, 2003); ISBN-10: 3540440011; ISBN-13: 978-3540440017.

Customer Relationship Management (Paperback) by Francis Buttle; 384 pages; Butterworth-Heinemann (December 3, 2003); ISBN-10: 075065502X; ISBN-13: 978-0750655026.

Guerrilla Marketing: Secrets for Making Big Profits from Your Small Business (Paperback) by Jay Conrad Levinson; 400 pages; Houghton Mifflin; 3 edition (October 21, 1998); ISBN-10: 0395906253; ISBN-13: 978-0395906255.

Harvard Business Review on Customer Relationship Management (Paperback) by C. K. Prahalad, Patrica B. Ramaswamy, Jon R. Katzenbach, Chris Lederer, Sam Hill; 224 pages; Harvard Business School Press; 1st edition (January 15, 2002); ISBN-10: 1578516994; ISBN-13: 978-1578516995.

How to Write a Marketing Plan (Creating Success) [ILLUSTRATED] (Paperback) by John Westwood; 129 pages; Kogan Page; 3 edition (September 1, 2006); ISBN-10: 0749445548; ISBN-13: 978-0749445546.

Marketing: An Introduction (8th Edition) by Gary Armstrong, Philip Kotler; 656 pages; Prentice Hall; 8 edition (February 27, 2006); ISBN-10: 0131865919; ISBN-13: 978-0131865914.

Marketing Management (12th Edition) (Hardcover) by Philip Kotler , Kevin Lane Keller; 816 pages; Prentice Hall; 12 edition (March 1, 2005); ISBN-10: 0131457578; ISBN-13: 978-0131457577.

Marketing Plan Workbook (Paperback) by John Westwood; 256 pages; Kogan Page (May 1, 2005); ISBN-10: 074944178X; ISBN-13: 978-0749441784.

Market Research: A Guide to Planning, Methodology and Evaluation (Paperback) by Paul Hague; 278 pages; Kogan Page; 3 edition (September 1, 2002); ISBN-10: 0749437308; ISBN-13: 978-0749437305.

Modern Competitive Analysis (Hardcover) by Sharon M. Oster; 448 pages; Oxford University Press, USA; 3 edition (March 19, 1999); ISBN-10: 019511941X; ISBN-13: 978-0195119411.

New Products Management (Cram101 Textbook Outlines – Textbook NOT Included) (Paperback) by Crawford, DiBenedetto; 300 pages; Academic Internet Publishers, Inc. (October 18, 2006); ISBN-10: 1428807411; ISBN-13: 978-1428807419.

Portfolio Management for New Products (Hardcover) by Robert G. Cooper, Scott J. Edgett, Elko J. Kleinschmidt; 288 pages; Perseus Books Group; 2nd edition (December 15, 2001); ISBN-10: 0738205141; ISBN-13: 978-0738205144.

Principles of Marketing (11th Edition) (Hardcover) by Philip Kotler, Gary Armstrong; 768 pages; Prentice Hall; 11 edition (February 1, 2005); ISBN-10: 0131469185; ISBN-13: 978-0131469181.

Product Strategy for High Technology Companies (Hardcover) by Michael E. McGrath; 400 pages; McGraw-Hill; 2nd edition (October 12, 2000); ISBN-10: 0071362460; ISBN-13: 978-0071362467.

Relationship Marketing: Gaining Competitive Advantage Through Customer Satisfaction and Customer Retention (Hardcover) by T., Hennig-Thurau, Thorsten, Hennig-Thurau, Ursula, Hansen; 484 pages; Springer Verlag GmbH; 1 edition (October 26, 2006); ISBN-10: 3540669426; ISBN-13: 978-3540669425.

State of The Art Marketing Research (Hardcover) by Albert Blankenship, George Breen, Alan Dutka; 454 pages; McGraw-Hill; 2 edition (June 11, 1998); ISBN-10: 0844234435; ISBN-13: 978-0844234434.

Strategic and Competitive Analysis: Methods and Techniques for Analysing Business Competition (Paperback) by Craig S. Fleisher, Babette Bensoussan; 457 pages; Prentice Hall; US Ed edition (March 29, 2002); ISBN-10: 0130888524; ISBN-13: 978-0130888525.

Successful Product Management (Sales & Marketing Series) (Paperback) by Stephen Morse; 150 pages; Kogan Page; 2 edition (July 1, 1998); ISBN-10: 0749427027; ISBN-13: 978-0749427023.

Sun Tzu Strategies for Winning the Marketing War: 12 Essential Principles for Winning the War for Customers (Paperback) by Gerald A. Michaelson, Steven W. Michaelson, Gerald Michaelson, Steven Michaelson ; Paperback: 200 pages; McGraw-Hill; 1 edition (October 20, 2003); ISBN-10: 0071427317; ISBN-13: 978-0071427319.

The CRM Handbook: A Business Guide to Customer Relationship Management (Paperback) by Jill Dyché; 336 pages; Addison-Wesley Professional; 1st edition (August 9, 2001); ISBN-10: 0201730626; ISBN-13: 978-0201730623.

The Customer Marketing Method: How To Implement and Profit from Customer Relationship Management (Hardcover) by Jay Curry, Adam Curry; 256 pages; Publisher: Free Press (March 27, 2000); ISBN-10: 0684839431; ISBN-13: 978-0684839431.

The Market Research Toolbox: A Concise Guide for Beginners Second Edition (Paperback) by Edward F. McQuarrie; 224 pages; Sage Publications, Inc; 2 edition (June 15, 2005); ISBN-10: 1412913195; ISBN-13: 978-1412913195.

The Product Manager's Field Guide : Practical Tools, Exercises, and Resources for Improved Product Management (Paperback) by Linda Gorchels; 228 pages; McGraw-Hill; 1 edition (April 28, 2003); ISBN-10: 0071410597; ISBN-13: 978-0071410595.

The Product Manager's Handbook, 3E (Hardcover) by Linda Gorchels; 389 pages; McGraw-Hill; 3 edition (November 7, 2005); ISBN-10: 0071459383; ISBN-13: 978-0071459389.

Qualitative Market Research: A Comprehensive Guide (Paperback) by Hy Mariampolski; 328 pages; Publisher: Sage Publications, Inc (August 21, 2001); ISBN-10: 0761969454; ISBN-13: 978-0761969457.

Questionnaire Design: How to Plan, Structure and Write Survey Material for Effective Market Research (Market Research in Practice Series) (Paperback) by Ian Brace; 289 pages; Kogan Page; Pap/Cdr edition (August 1, 2004); ISBN-10: 074944181X; ISBN-13: 978-0749441814.

Chapter 9-11

Business Logistics: Supply Chain Management (Hardcover) by Ronald H. Ballou; 816 pages; Prentice Hall; 5 edition (August 21, 2003); ISBN-10: 0130661848; ISBN-13: 978-0130661845.

Contemporary Logistics, Eighth Edition (Hardcover) by Paul R. Murphy, Donald Wood; 544 pages; Prentice Hall; 8 edition (July 10, 2003); ISBN-10: 0130352802; ISBN-13: 978-0130352804.

Controller's Guide to Planning and Controlling Operations (Hardcover) by Steven M. Bragg; 384 pages; Wiley (February 9, 2004); ISBN-10: 0471576808; ISBN-13: 978-0471576808.

Essentials of Supply Chain Management, 2nd Edition (Paperback) by Michael Hugos; 304 pages; Wiley; 2 edition (March 10, 2006); ISBN-10: 0471776343; ISBN-13: 978-0471776345.

Fourth Generation R&D: Managing Knowledge, Technology, and Innovation (Hardcover); by William L. Miller, Langdon Morris; 368

pages; Wiley; 1 edition (August 16, 1999); ISBN-10: 0471240931; ISBN-13: 978-0471240938.

Fundamentals of Logistics Management (Paperback) by David Grant, Douglas M. Lambert, James R. Stock, Lisa M. Ellram; 512 pages; McGraw Hill Higher Education; European ed edition (October 1, 2005); ISBN-10: 0077108949; ISBN-13: 978-0077108946.

Fundamentals of Production Planning and Control (Paperback) by Stephen N. Chapman; 288 pages; Prentice Hall (March 1, 2005); ISBN-10: 013017615X; ISBN-13: 978-0130176158.

Harvard Business Review on Supply Chain Management (Harvard Business Review Paperback Series) (Paperback); 211 pages; Harvard Business School Press; 1 edition (August 28, 2006); ISBN-10: 1422102793; ISBN-13: 978-1422102794.

Introduction to Materials Management (5th Edition) (Hardcover) by J.R. Tony Arnold, Stephen N. Chapman; 480 pages; Prentice Hall; 5 edition (July 29, 2003); ISBN-10: 0131128744; ISBN-13: 978-0131128743.

Logistics & Supply Chain Management: creating value-adding networks (3rd Edition) (Hardcover) by Martin Christopher; 320 pages; FT Press; 3 edition (February 14, 2005); ISBN-10: 0273681761; ISBN-13: 978-0273681762.

Management of Business Logistics: A Supply Chain Perspective (Hardcover) by John J. Coyle, Edward J. Bardi, C. John Langley; South-Western College Pub; 7 edition (January 22, 2002); ISBN-10: 0324007515; ISBN-13: 978-0324007510.

Management of Research and Development Organizations: Managing the Unmanageable, 2nd Edition (Hardcover) by R. K. Jain, Harry C. Triandis; 336 pages; Wiley-Interscience; 2nd edition (December 16, 1996); ISBN-10: 0471146137; ISBN-13: 978-0471146131.

Manufacturing Planning and Control Systems for Supply Chain Management: The Definitive Guide for Professionals (Hardcover) by Thomas E Vollmann, William Lee Berry, David Clay Whybark, F. Robert Jacobs, Thomas Vollmann, William Berry; 598 pages; McGraw-Hill; 5 edition (April 1, 2004); ISBN-10: 007144033X; ISBN-13: 978-0071440332.

Optimal Flow Control in Manufacturing Systems: Production Planning and Scheduling (Hardcover) by O. Maimon, E. Khmelnitsky, K. Kogan; 360 pages; Springer; 1 edition (August 31, 1998); ISBN-10: 0792351061; ISBN-13: 978-0792351061.

Planning and Scheduling of Production Systems: Methodologies and applications (Hardcover) by A. Artiba, S.E. Elmaghraby; 384 pages; Springer; 1 edition (December 31, 1996); ISBN-10: 0412610205; ISBN-13: 978-0412610202.

Portfolio Management for New Products (Hardcover) by Robert G. Cooper, Scott J. Edgett, Elko J. Kleinschmidt; 288 pages; Perseus Books Group; 2nd edition (December 15, 2001); ISBN-10: 0738205141; ISBN-13: 978-0738205144.

Practical Production Control: A Survival Guide for Planners and Schedulers (Hardcover) by Kenneth N. McKay, Vincent C. S. Wiers; 269 pages; J. Ross Publishing (August 2004); ISBN-10: 1932159304; ISBN-13: 978-1932159301.

Strategic Supply Chain Alignment: Best Practice in Supply Chain Management (Hardcover) by John Gattorna; 671 pages; Gower Publishing Company; 6Rev Ed edition (July 1998); ISBN-10: 0566078252; ISBN-13: 978-0566078255.

The Smart Organization: Creating Value Through Strategic R&D (Hardcover) by David Matheson, James E. Matheson; 292 pages; Harvard Business School Press (January 1998); ISBN-10: 087584765X; ISBN-13: 978-0875847658.

The Valuation of Technology: Business and Financial Issues in R&D (Operations Management Series) (Hardcover) by F. Peter Boer; 432 pages; Wiley; Bk & Disk edition (February 26, 1999); ISBN-10: 0471316385; ISBN-13: 978-0471316381.

Chapter 12

Accounting for Managers (Briefcase Books Series) (Paperback) by William Webster; 225 pages; McGraw-Hill; 1 edition (October 1, 2003); ISBN-10: 0071421742; ISBN-13: 978-0071421744.

Best Practices in Planning and Performance Management: From Data to Decisions (Wiley Best Practices) (Hardcover) by David A. J. Axson; 288 pages; Wiley; 2 edition (January 9, 2007); ISBN-10: 0470008571; ISBN-13: 978-0470008577.

Budgeting for Managers (Paperback) by Sid Kemp, Eric Dunbar; 180 pages; McGraw-Hill; 1 edition (January 30, 2003); ISBN-10: 0071391339; ISBN-13: 978-0071391337.

Enterprise Risk Management: From Incentives to Controls (Hardcover) by James Lam 336 pages; Wiley; 1ST edition (May 16, 2003); ISBN-10: 0471430005; ISBN-13: 978-0471430001.

Financial Analysis Tools and Techniques: A Guide for Managers (Hardcover) by Erich A. Helfert; 480 pages; McGraw-Hill; 1 edition (September 11, 2001); ISBN-10: 0071378340; ISBN-13: 978-0071378345.

Finance for Managers (Harvard Business Essentials) (Paperback) by Harvard Business School Press; 256 pages; Harvard Business School Press (February 2002); ISBN-10: 1578518768; ISBN-13: 978-1578518760.

Financial Planning using Excel: Forecasting, Planning and Budgeting Techniques (CIMA Professional Handbook) (Paperback); 192 pages; CIMA Publishing; Pap/Cdr edition (December 8, 2005); ISBN-10: 0750663553; ISBN-13: 978-0750663557.

Making Enterprise Risk Management Pay Off: How Leading Companies Implement Risk Management (Paperback) by Thomas L. Barton, William G. Shenkir , Paul L. Walker; 272 pages; FT Press; 1st edition (February 8, 2002); ISBN-10: 0130087548; ISBN-13: 978-0130087546.

Performance Management (Paperback) by Robert Bacal; 160 pages; McGraw-Hill; 1 edition (November 30, 1998); ISBN-10: 0070718660; ISBN-13: 978-0070718661.

The Balanced Scorecard: Translating Strategy into Action (Hardcover) by Robert S. Kaplan, David P. Norton; 322 pages; Harvard Business School Press (September 1996); ISBN-10: 0875846513; ISBN-13: 978-0875846514.

The Essentials of Risk Management (Hardcover) by Michel Crouhy, Dan Galai, Robert Mark; 416 pages; McGraw-Hill; 1 edition (December 14, 2005); ISBN-10: 0071429662; ISBN-13: 978-0071429665.

The Quick Guide to Small Business Budgeting (Spiral-bound) by Julie Mucha-aydlott; 102 pages; San Diego Business Accounting Solutions (June 21, 2005); ISBN-10: 097460934X; ISBN-13: 978-0974609348.

Total Business Budgeting: A Step-by-Step Guide with Forms, 2nd Edition (Hardcover) by Robert Rachlin; 321 pages; Wiley; 2 edition (August 27, 1999); ISBN-10: 0471351032; ISBN-13: 978-0471351030.

Chapter 13

Attracting Equity Investors: Positioning, Preparing, and Presenting the Business Plan (Paperback) by Dean A. Shepherd , Evan J. Douglas; 192 pages, Sage Publications, Inc (December 21, 1998); ISBN-10: 0761914773; ISBN-13: 978-0761914778.

Attracting Investors: A Marketing Approach to Finding Funds for Your Business (Hardcover) by Philip Kotler, Hermawan Kartajaya, S. David Young; 256 pages; Publisher: Wiley (August 13, 2004); ISBN-10: 0471646563; ISBN-13: 978-0471646563.

About the authors

Gerald Schwetje, holding a diploma in commerce, is a managing partner at the Hamburger Beratungs-Kontor GmbH & Co. KG in Hamburg. Mr. Schwetje has concentrated on consulting middle-class companies in strategy, organization and technology in manufacturing, consumer business and service industry. Before his time at the Hamburger Beratungs-Kontor he worked for Deloitte & Touche and Deloitte Consulting. There he was a partner and ran the consumer business area, where he was in charge of numerous customers from the trade and consumer goods areas. Before that Mr. Schwetje worked as a leading consultant at IBM management consulting, where he concentrated on "Business Transformation" and "Strategy and Planning of Information Systems". He has over 15 years of professional experience. In the field of management, sales and marketing he has been able to gain his experience during 10 years of management at IBM and Digital. Mr. Schwetje has carried out numerous business plan projects in middle-class companies, he has given lectures and he has organized events concerning this topic.

Dr. Sam Vaseghi completed his studies of Mechanical Engineering, Process Engineering (MSc) and Biology (MSc) at the technological University in Stuttgart, where he then worked as an engineer (Dr. Ing.) in the faculty of process engineering. In the 90s he worked in the fields of Software Engineering and Work Organization at the renowned Institute of Work Economy and Organization of the Frauenhofer Company in Stuttgart. In the following years he worked for renowned customers such as AOL, Time Warner, CompuServe, Netscape, mobilcom and France Telecom in the fields of Software Engineering, Infrastructural Development and Business Development. He developed his career as consultant at the EDS Consulting Group in the field of E- and M-Business, and later in the Management Consulting of Deloitte in Hamburg. Since 2005 Dr. Vaseghi has been working in the department of Global Environment and Sustainability Services of Deloitte in Copenhagen. From there he has been taking charge of clients worldwide in the fields of Sustainable Business and Sustainability Reporting. Renowned companies such as BASF, Bayer, Lufthansa, OMV, Grundfos, Toyota Motor Europe, Sonae Indústria und Vodafone, among others, belong to his clients. In 2006 he gained qualifications within the Deloitte Leadership programme with the Harvard Business School.

Printing: Krips bv, Meppel
Binding: Stürtz, Würzburg